The Mystery of Firstfruits

by Doctor Carlos Williams

xulon PRESS

The Mystery of Firstfruits
By Doctor Carlos Williams

Printed in the United States of America

ISBN 1-594673-81-0

Editor: Tom Gill

www.xulonpress.com

Aknowledgements

To my father Archbishop Dr. Charles Wesley Williams Sr. who has gone on to be with the Lord and to my mother Lady Eartha Williams who instilled biblical principles within me and led me to Christ at an early age. You raised me in a loving home with three other siblings, Bishop Dr. Deborah W. Belton, Pastor Sophia J. Williams, and Leland Williams. Thank you for building a solid platform from which I was to be launched into the world.

To my beautiful wife Marie, You are my perfect gift from God and with out you I would not know that a marriage could be like heaven on earth. Thanks for all you've done to make this possible, I Love you always and forever.

To my daughters Lawanda and Moriel, thanks for the joy it is in being your father and the time you two have afforded me in completing this project.

To my spiritual father and mother Dr. and Mrs. Leroy Thompson Sr. You have impacted my life in ways that you will never know. Pace setters, barrier breakers, Pioneers, and champions of the cause righteousness; Thanks for being that living example of the abundant life that God desires for all his children.

To Life House Church, what a pleasure it is to be affiliated with extra ordinary people like you. Thank for all the encouragement, kindness and respectfulness. God will reward you mightily.

Table of Contents

Introduction

—————

Over the years, there has been a shift in the body of Christ in the giving of tithes and offerings. For many years, the church had been taught that the principle of tithing – returning a tenth to the Lord – was an Old Testament principle and was not required. Other offerings, including the Firstfruit Offering, were looked at in the same way and deemed unnecessary.

God allowed this heresy to flourish until men and women of God began to question why the church was broke, hungry, weak and ineffective. As these pioneer saints pressed in to God, they began to hear Him talk about offering our first and best to Him. They heard Him say that He had offered His first and best to us in Christ Jesus so we should offer our best to Him.

This "new" teaching was met with ridicule and downright meanness in the body of Christ. Preachers of this message paid a dear price to get the word out that God wanted to bless His children, not see them live in poverty and despair. Many of these preachers were cut-off from the associations they once belonged to; denominations withdrew support and even cast some of them out; churches became divided and some even split because of the truth being taught.

Nevertheless, the message continued to be preached – God's determination would not be thwarted.

Fruit cannot be hidden. Therefore, as the preachers of prosperity began to bear fruit and the members in their churches began to prosper, the body of Christ began to take notice. Today, the message of biblical prosperity is known throughout the church.

Today, we are witnessing a supernatural transfer of wealth from the kingdom of darkness into the Kingdom of Light. The wealth of the wicked is truly laid up for the righteous and it's beginning to come in. The church is no longer groveling and begging for a handout. Instead, the church is blessing those who encounter her as she takes her rightful place in this world.

This book is offered to the body of Christ as an additional testimony of God's desire for His people to prosper and His church to reign triumphant. Firstfruits offerings are our response to the promises of God in His Word. Furthermore, firstfruits offerings express where our hope for the future is found... in God and God alone.

This book will unlock the secrets of firstfruits giving and show you how to appropriate the promises of God. You'll learn that...

- God Himself offered Firstfruits
- The second major attack on humanity was in the giving of firstfruits
- Freedom comes through firstfruits giving
- Prosperity awaits those who give firstfruits
- The Power is in Your Hands

Take time to read this book carefully. Many truths of God's Word that unlock the secrets of firstfruits giving are covered in these pages. Then, when you've taken it all in and are living a firstfruits life, share it with another person.

I know you'll be blessed as you apply the principles set forth in this book. Furthermore, I know that God's hand will move on your behalf as you establish His Word in your life through firstfruits giving. Remember, you're blessed to be a blessing, so spread it around. Sow your seed and reap an abundant harvest.

CHAPTER 1

The Truth About Firstfruits

I have been on a quest. For many years, I've believed and taught that God wants His children to prosper. I've read the promises of Scripture that declare God's children will be the head and not the tail, will be blessed in basket and store and will be blessed going in and coming out (Deut. 28:1-15). I've taught that each day we have the choice of whether to live in blessing or curse (Deut. 11:26-27) and that life or death is set before us each day (Deut. 30:15).

However, something was missing in all the teaching. My obedience was there and I believe the Word of the Lord but somehow, I was missing it.

Where Is The Abundance Promised?

There used to be a commercial on TV showing a little old lady buying a hamburger and then shouting, "Where's the beef?" She expected to bite into the bun and get a good portion of meat but got only bread. For a time, "Where's the beef?" became a slogan for those who didn't get what was advertised or what was expected.

Like the lady in the commercial, I found myself asking God, "Where's the abundance?" I wanted to know why things weren't turning out like the Word said they should. Why weren't my circumstances lining up with the Word of God? The promises were there along with the commandment to serve the Lord. I thought I was living up to my end, but it seemed like God wasn't.

I wanted to shout at God and say, "Where is this abundant life that Jesus came to give" but I knew deep inside myself that the problem had to be with me, not God. I was missing something, not God.

The Bible says, "Beloved, I wish above all things that thou mayest prosper and be in health, even as thy soul prospereth" (3 John 1:2). I knew that John wrote that verse under the inspiration of the Holy Ghost and that God doesn't say anything unless He means it. Furthermore, I knew that my soul was prospering because of the truth and reality of my salvation in Christ Jesus. I just had to discover why I wasn't prospering in other areas of my life.

Robbing God

The prophet, Malachi, declared, "Will a man rob God? Yet ye have robbed me. But ye say, Wherein have we robbed thee? In tithes and offerings" (Mal. 3:8).

I searched my life and obedience and really believed that in no way had I robbed God. I can remember as a child being given a dollar for allowance, putting ten cents in the plate as tithe and fifteen cents in for offering. I was giving 25% of what I had been given as tithes and offerings. Because I was taught the importance of this from my youth, it continued into adulthood. I love to give.

The Bible teaches that God loves a cheerful giver (2 Cor. 9:7). I am a cheerful giver. I understand the truth that all I have comes from God. I know the importance of returning to the Lord a tenth or tithe of all that I get. Furthermore, I understand the importance of offerings over and above the tithe. In fact, it's in the offering that the blessing comes. The tithe is a requirement, offerings bring blessing.

As I prayed over this and sought the Lord for insight, understanding began to come. All of my life I had been robbing God because I didn't understand a very important principle of giving.

The Curse of Disobedience

Malachi went on to declare, "Ye *are* cursed with a curse: for ye have robbed me, *even* this whole nation" (Mal. 3:9). God showed me that I was not walking in blessing because of disobedience. I must tell you that if you're not walking in blessing, you're walking in the curse. There is no middle ground.

When this understanding came to me, I cried out to God to show me where I had missed it. I wanted to know so I could be fully His and not out from under the shadow of His wings of blessing and security.

The answer began to come while I was reading in Genesis chapter 4:

> And in process of time it came to pass, that Cain brought of the fruit of the ground an offering unto the LORD. And Abel, he also brought of the firstlings of his flock and of the fat thereof. And the LORD had respect unto Abel and to his offering:

But unto Cain and to his offering he had not respect.
And Cain was very wroth, and his countenance fell.
(Gen. 4:3-5)

After reading this, I began to wonder why God accepted Abel's offering and not Cain's. I had heard before that it was because Abel offered an animal while Cain offered fruit of the ground. But, that didn't make any sense. Both brought what they did. Why would God accept one and refuse another.

Firstlings

The more I studied these three verses, the more convinced I became that Abel's offering was accepted because he brought the firstborn, the firstlings of his flock. Cain, on the other hand, brought "of the fruit of the ground." Nothing here indicates that Cain brought the first or the best of what he had grown.

This understanding led me deeper into the Word of God as I searched for answers. I saw that the firstborn or firstfruit was designated holy by God in the Law and demonstrated as holy in Jesus. I learned that God requires the firstlings of not only the flocks and herds, but of His people as well. The firstborn must be consecrated unto Him. I also learned that God demonstrated obedience to His own Word by the offering of Jesus as firstfruit.

What and Why?

I desperately wanted to know more and to find answers for

these questions:

1. What is it about the firstborn or firstfruit that is more acceptable than the rest?
2. Why would a firstfruit offering be of more value than any other offering?
3. How do we give firstfruit offerings today?

Each of these questions will be answered in more detail later on in the book, but here is a brief answer that will give you an idea where we're headed.

What is it about the firstborn or firstfruits that is more acceptable than the rest?

Couples wait with eager anticipation for the birth of their first baby. Farmers check the field daily when it comes time for their crops to bear fruit. Ranchers keep watch over their flocks and herds as the birthing time draws near, especially with animals that have never given birth.

The anticipation of and newness of birth always draws our attention and captures our imagination. We see in the fruit of the field, vine, and womb hope for the future and purpose for being.

When farmers see the firstfruit and hold it in their hands, they sense that the value of the crop surpasses any expectation they had at seedtime. When ranchers behold a newborn lamb or calf, the promise of renewal and growth launches them into the future. When couples hold their newborn baby son or daughter, suddenly the joy and responsiblility of parenting and future hopes and dreams for the family becomes vivid in their mind's eye.

Firstfruits are more valuable because of the promise of the future portrayed by them. We know that the future is in God's hands, so firstfruits point us directly to God. First so we can thank Him for giving us a future, and second because we want Him to have our best.

Why would a firstfruit offering be of more value than any other offering?

The firstfruit offering is more valuable because of the promise attached to it. All of our future increase, provision, wealth, health and prosperity is tied to the firstfruit offering. We proclaim with that offering that God...

- is sovereign
- holds our destiny in His hand
- seeks our best as we give our best
- gave His best in Jesus Christ

The value is not tied to the worldly worth of what is offered. Instead, the value is determined by the future the offering proclaims.

How do we give firstfruit offerings today?

Today we give firstfruits in much the same way as in days of old. The only difference is in <u>what</u> we give. In days past, the first portion of the harvest was given, the first bull or first ram born.

Today, we give the first of whatever is new and on going. Business owners may give the proceeds of the first sale or individuals may give the first portion of a raise they've earned.

Honor God With Your Money

Firstfruits giving is an expression of dependence on God unlike any other offering. Giving firstfruits makes a declaration that more is on the way. Too often, we give out of obligation instead of anticipation. Firstfruits giving shatters that mindset and focuses our attention on God and God's promises.

Giving firstfruits honors God by declaring that he is in charge of your future. Think of it like this: In most cases when you buy something on credit, you are gambling that you'll have the money in the future to pay for what you've charged. Giving a firstfruits offering recognizes that God has set a harvest in your life that He is overseeing. It's the opposite of buying on credit and hoping something will be there to pay the bill. Firstfruits giving establishes the future in prosperity whereas credit robs you of your future increase.

The Bible declares that we must seek God and His Kingdom First, in all that we do (Matt. 6:33). As we do so, the promise is that everything will be added to us that we need. Jesus made it very clear in the Sermon on the Mount (Matt. 5-7) that we must not worry about tomorrow. Too much debt causes us to worry about where the money will come from to fulfill our obligations. Jesus further said that we couldn't serve both God and mammon (Matt. 6:24). Therefore, our responsibility is to God first. As we seek Him and His righteousness our needs are met and mammon (money) is brought under control. You simply serve God and Master your money.

The Firstfruits Are Holy

The apostle Paul declared, "For if the firstfruit *be* holy, the lump *is* also *holy*: and if the root *be* holy, so *are* the branches" (Rom. 11:16). Paul is talking about the Lord Jesus Christ as the Firstfruits and the Root. The prophet Isaiah declared, "And in that day there shall be a root of Jesse, which shall stand for an ensign of the people; to it shall the Gentiles seek: and his rest shall be glorious" (Isaiah 11:10).

Therefore, if the root is good, the branches will be good. Likewise, if the firstfruits are holy, then the lump or the remainder is also holy. Jesus is the Firstfruits of God. We are in Christ and so have become the "lump." Therefore, because Christ Jesus is holy, we are holy. This holiness is not because of what we've done or who we've been. It's because of whose we are and in whom we are – Jesus.

Holiness is imputed to us based on the finished work of Jesus. Therefore, we are holy because He is holy. Because Jesus is the Firstfruits, which is holy, then we, as the lump or residue, are holy.

Likewise, when we, being holy because of Christ's holiness, offer our firstfruits (which is holy) to God, so the lump or residue of what we have is holy. This means that if you are getting a $50 per week raise and you give the first $50 as a firstfruits offering, the remainder of that raise, for as long as it's coming in, is holy. That money is blessed. That money is marked as holy money.

Imagine if you had done that to your first paycheck when you first started. Then all the money you earn would be holy money. All of your check would be holy unto God and blessed by the Almighty. Imagine what you could do with blessed money!

Remember, the Lord declared in Malachi 3:8 that by not giving tithes and offerings you rob God. That means that all your money is cursed until you begin to honor God with it.

Blessed money is that which follows the firstfruits offering. It's blessed because the firstfruits are holy making the lump or residue holy.

The Truth About Firstfruits Offerings

In this chapter we've begun to expose the truth about firstfruits offerings. You've read that firstfruits giving…

- unleashes the power of God on your finances.
- opens the door of heaven so God can pour His blessing upon you the blessings.
- prepares the way to receive the blessing of God.

Open your heart today to receive what God has for you. Prayerfully submit to Him the firstfruits of all that you have and will receive. I guarantee that you'll not regret it for one moment. God has set His hand to move on your behalf. All I can tell you is, "The struggle is over." "Get ready." "It's your time". To live the abundant life that Jesus came to give to all who believe.

CHAPTER 2

A Higher Level of Giving

I'm pressing on the upward way
New heights I'm gaining every day
Still praying as I'm onward bound
"Lord plant my feet on higher ground"

My heart has no desire to stay
Where doubts arise and fears dismay
Tho' some may dwell where these abound
My prayer, my aim, is higher ground

I want to scale the utmost height
And catch a gleam of glory bright
But still I'll pray till Heav'n I've found
"Lord, lead me on to higher ground"

Chorus
Lord lift me up and let me stand
By faith, on Heaven's table land
A higher plane than I have found
Lord plant my feet on higher ground[1]

This old hymn expresses the desire of most Christians in their walk with the Lord. Our walk by faith must lead somewhere or else we're going no where. The world thinks it's going somewhere and plans are made everyday to speed its arrival. However, without Christ, the world's somewhere is no where.

God has set your feet on a path and aimed you in a direction that leads directly to His throne. His desire for you is success and plenty, not failure and lack. Therefore, to speed you on your way, God has set in place certain principles in His Word. These principles are for your benefit and will strengthen your walk in the Lord as you apply them to your life.

I'm Going Somewhere

If you desire to take a trip, it's important to know where you're going. If you don't know where you are going, how will you know if you ever get there? If you walk up to the airline ticket counter to buy a ticket, the agent will ask you where you want to go. If you don't tell them where but insist on buying a ticket, you are just about guaranteed a trip and a wardrobe for the place you will be taken.

Likewise with God's Word. Jesus promised not to leave us as orphans, but sent the Holy Spirit to live in and through us. Because the Holy Spirit is just as much God as the Father and the Son, He knows where He's going and how to take us along.

I'm going somewhere. I'm on the same journey that the apostle Paul was on when he said, "but *this* one thing *I do*, forgetting those things which are behind, and reaching forth unto those things which are before, I press toward the mark for the prize of the high calling of God in Christ Jesus" (Phil 3:13-14). I'm moving upward on the path to higher ground.

Firstfruits giving is part of the journey. God has shown through His Word the importance of firstfruits, we learned about it in the last chapter. Now we'll examine the difference between firstfruits and tithes.

Tithes and Offerings

The tithe is holy and belongs to the Lord (Lev. 27:30,32). Because the tithe is holy, it must be treated with utmost respect and honor.

The Hebrew word for tithe is *ma`aser* and means, "tenth" or "payment of a tenth part." Likewise, the Greek word for tithe, *apodekatoo*, means tenth. Therefore, in both the Old and New Testaments, to tithe means the same thing – giving one tenth.

The next question most people ask is, "One tenth of what? Gross or net?" The Bible simply says one tenth. Therefore, taken in context, it becomes very clear that it is one tenth of the gross. For example, shepherds would count their flocks and give a tithe to the Lord. To count the sheep, the shepherd would hold a rod over the path leading into the pen, counting each one as it passed under the rod. The total number that passed under the rod was then used to determine the tenth (Lev. 27:32). If you give tithe on the gross and if you get an income tax check you are only required to give an offering of it because you already paid tithes on that money.

Tithing removes the curse from the money that passes through your hands. The prophet, Malachi, declared:

> Will a man rob God? Yet ye have robbed me. But ye

say, Wherein have we robbed thee? In tithes and offerings.

Ye *are* cursed with a curse: for ye have robbed me, *even* this whole nation.

Bring ye all the tithes into the storehouse, that there may be meat in mine house, and prove me now herewith, saith the LORD of hosts, if I will not open you the windows of heaven, and pour you out a blessing, that *there shall* not *be room* enough *to receive it.*

And I will rebuke the devourer for your sakes, and he shall not destroy the fruits of your ground; neither shall your vine cast her fruit before the time in the field, saith the LORD of hosts.

And all nations shall call you blessed: for ye shall be a delightsome land, saith the LORD of hosts. (Mal. 3:8-12)

By not tithing, Israel had come under a curse. However, God declared that as they brought their tithes into the storehouse, He would open the windows of heaven and pour out a blessing over them. For years in teaching on tithes I have said that to Rob someone is to cause a depletion of their resources. Ergo, No one could put a gun to God's back and say "stick em up". God never runs out. He is the God of increase. Then how can we rob God? Well while at a conference the guest speaker (Dr Leroy Thompson), made a statement that I will never forget. He told us to turn to Psalms 35:27. It reads "Let them shout for joy, and be glad, that favour my righteous cause: yea, let them say continually, Let the LORD be magnified, which hath pleasure in the prosperity of his servant." He then explained that when we choose to with hold our tithes, we rob

God of the Pleasure of prospering us. Any true father wants to bless his children.

Offerings are given over and above tithes. The tithe is holy and belongs to God, while offerings are voluntarily given to God out of our heart in love. Everything we have comes from God. Though God may use a job and an employer to bless us, it all comes from Him nonetheless.

When this understanding finally pierces our heart and penetrates our mind, it changes the way we view our paycheck, our job, and our employer. Suddenly, instead of being agents of hardship and despair they become channels of God's blessing.

Knowledge of these principles of giving is critical to properly understand not only tithes, but firstfruits as well. Being obedient to God in the tithe brings blessing. Likewise, being obedient to God in firstfruits giving brings blessing as well.

Submission – The Key To Firstfruit Giving

Obedience is the hallmark of giving both tithes and offerings. Before you can enter into the fullness of God's promises, you must be obedient to Him. Obedience brings blessing but rebellion brings curse (Deut. 11:26-28).

Obedience is submission to an authority greater than you are. Submission to God means that you have surrendered your arms of rebellion and have allowed God to have full control in your life. This is what it means to call Jesus "Lord."

Remember, biblical firstfruits were the firstlings of a flock or first harvest of a crop or field. Today, unless you're a farmer or rancher, firstfruits could be the first check from a new job or the first payment of a raise you have been given or your first paycheck of the new year. Well you say I get paid twice a month what is my first fruit? It could be your first week of your first check of the new year. If you open a business the first fruit would be your first sale. In many business you see the first "dollars" made on the wall. The first fruit doesn't belong to the wall it belongs to the Lord. If you want it on the wall copy it but give the first fruit to God so that the 'blessing' can rest in your house. You could be self employed and are paid daily; your first fruit could be your first day's pay of the new year. – any amount that is on-going is subject to firstfruits giving. By now you noticed that there appears to be discrepancies in the amount of the first fruits. In some cases for those who are paid bi-weekly I have stated that it could be the whole first check of a new job or it could be just the first week. It could be the first of paid wages. You are actually paid by the day. It is a well- known fact that if you leave a job before the pay week is finished you will not be paid for the days that you did not work.   The person who gives the first fruit decides what it will be, because this is an act of faith. One person's first fruit could be there entire first check of a new job or of the New Year. Another person's first fruit could be the first week's pay of a new job or of the New Year. You must stand on your own two faith feet.

You may be thinking, "Dr. Williams. That could be a lot of money! The first check of my new job? The first payment of my new raise? Are you sure?"

This is why submission is so critical to this principle. When the enemy comes after you, how often does he hit your finances? How often do you submit to the devil when it comes to your money instead of to God? "I can't afford to tithe this week. The electric bill is due." You can't afford not to tithe! Take your money out of the devil's hands and put it into God's!

Submission to God is critical, because obedience to Him and His statutes is the avenue of blessing.

Firstfruits Offerings Are Given To God Through The Priest

I heard of a business owner who not only was a tither but he also after hearing the message on first fruit, decided to give first fruit. It is said that one January he decided to give the first week of the as first fruit to his pastor. Well he did it despite much pressure from the devil to back away from this revelation. On the fourth week of that same month the income of his business was over three times as much as the first weeks income and that year was the greatest financial year for the his company. Why did he give his first fruit to their pastor? Because his pastor is the one who will receive the firstfruits offering and wave it before the Lord so the blessing will rest in business owner's house.

When he sowed firstfruits into their his pastor, it's was as if they had given it to the priest. The priest then takes the offering and waves it before the Lord on behalf of those who gave it. This act unleashes the blessing of God on the giver.

God challenged the people in Malachi 3:10 to: "Bring ye all the tithes into the storehouse, that there may be meat in mine house, and <u>prove me now herewith, saith the LORD of hosts</u>, if I will not open you the windows of heaven, and pour you out (A) blessing, that *there shall* not *be room* enough *to receive it*" (Mal. 3:10). God is actually challenging you to prove Him or test Him according to His promise. Do you believe God? Will you prove God in the area of First Fruits also? Note: the Pastor is likened to the Priest of the local church. And a Spiritual father of the Pastor would be likened to the Priest of the Pastor.

Sowing For The Harvest – The Blessing of God

Farmers plant seed so they can reap a harvest. Likewise, according to the Scripture above, we can sow tithes and offerings to receive a blessing from God. What is that blessing?

The blessing promised is more than just a financial return on what was sown. Yes, God does promise a 30, 60, 100, 1000 fold and unlimited return on your sowing, but this blessing is different.

The blessing of God cannot be likened to money, houses, cars, boats, airplanes, or anything temporal. When you walk in the blessing of God, every aspect of your life is affected – health, wealth, relationships, ministry, employment, family, etc. God blesses all of your life, not just a part of it. The blessing is the ability to prosper in every area of your life. It is Divine favor that is draped on you like a coat. Yes you actually wear the blessing.

Scripture declares that you must, "...remember the LORD thy God: for *it is* he that giveth thee power to get wealth, that he may establish his covenant..." (Deut. 8:18). The blessing is important because through it, God establishes His covenant of salvation and uses you as a willing participant!

Sadly, some people don't understand why God blesses them. It's not so that they can accumulate more and more wealth just to hoard it up, it's so they can help God's covenant to be established and to be a blessing to others. Likewise, you are blessed to be a blessing.

Don't put limits on God or what He wants to do in and through your life. As you submit to Him, He begins to work things in and through you that you would not have been able to do on your own.

God is greater than any person or thing and His ways are higher. Therefore, as He moves obstacles are swept out of the way and His will is accomplished in His way.

A Higher Level of Giving

Giving your firstfruits opens windows of heaven that may have remained shut even though you were faithful in the tithe. It's a different, higher level of giving than even the tithe. Firstfruit giving means that instead of looking at the harvest after it's been gathered in, you look at the harvest before it's even come in – and then give on it!

Giving firstfruits leads you into prophetic giving based on what God will do, not merely on what he has done. When you begin to give prophetically, you open yourself to realms of God's glory that embolden you even more. You begin to see that no matter how much you give in obedience to God, you can never out-give Him.

You also begin to see what you've sown bear fruit. Too often, Christians give so they can see a building built. Prophetic giving opens the realm of seeing cities and nations rebuilt for God. God is glorified as He magnifies your firstfruits to bring about His purpose on earth.

Higher levels of giving lead to higher levels of living. Begin in submission with the tithe, and God will move you toward giving offerings. Stay in submission with tithes and offerings, and God will move you toward giving of the firstfruits. When that happens, look out! God is positioning you to receive more than you could imagine. The apostle Paul declared that if you can think about it, you are not close to what your Heavenly Father wants to do for you: "Now unto him that is able to do exceeding abundantly above all that we ask or think…" (Eph. 3:20).

How big is your mind? God is bigger! So take hold of Him and hang on. The ride is unlike anything you've ever experienced.

---

[1] "Higher Ground" Copyright, 1926, Homer A. Rodehaver

CHAPTER 3

Faith Overcomes Fear

—————>•<—————

Herein is our love made perfect, that we may have boldness in the day of judgment: because as he is, so are we in this world. There is no fear in love; but perfect love casteth out fear: because fear hath torment. He that feareth is not made perfect in love. (1 John 4:17-18)

This Scripture is crucial to your understanding of the importance of firstfruits giving. Verse eighteen declares that fear brings torment and that fear keeps you from being made perfect in love.

We discussed in the last chapter that the enemy often attacks finances to keep you from honoring God with your resources. These attacks often result in the fear of losing all that you have worked hard to accumulate.

Sadly, many Christians think that their job, boss, family, or inheritance is their source instead of God. Therefore, any attack that threatens the stability or availability of income from that source throws them into a tailspin and takes their eyes off God.

I AM THAT I AM

When God spoke His name to Moses He revealed something of Himself that transcended everything Moses had ever known. "And God said unto Moses, I AM THAT I AM: and he said, Thus shalt thou say unto the children of Israel, I AM hath sent me unto you" (Exodus 3:14).

When God said to Moses, "I AM THAT I AM" He declared the fact of His eternal existence. This is important because nothing existed before God. The Bible declares that, "In the beginning God created the heaven and the earth" (Gen. 1:1). Therefore, everything in the created order came from God.

Sin entered into creation first with Lucifer (Isaiah 14:12-15) and then in the Garden of Eden with Adam and Eve (Gen. 3:1-7). With sin came fear that began gnawing at the tether binding God and man together, finally severing it. With the tether cut, a wide gulf opened between man and God that wasn't spanned until Jesus Christ gave His life on Calvary and ascended into Heaven.

God's declaration of His identity to Moses was the first step on a long journey for Moses. This journey culminated in the freedom of Israel from slavery in Egypt and their crossing the Jordan to possess their inheritance.

During that forty-year span, Moses learned the value of depending completely on God and not on his own strength. Moses' life was in God's hand and he knew it. At any time, God could have abandoned Moses and left him and the Israelites alone in the desert. However, because of God's faithful adherence to His covenant with Abraham and promises to Moses, the people were set free to begin again in a new land.

Overcoming The Slave Mentality

Moses was given the responsibility of leading a people who had been in slavery their entire lives. This group of slaves had never known freedom, nor had their parents. At one time, Israel was revered in Egypt, but that reputation had long passed.

Slaves have one thing in common – they have no say in what to do or where to go. Every activity of slaves is directed by a slave master who tells them where to go, what to do, and when they're finished. Furthermore, slave masters rarely care about the men and women under their care. To them, they are no more than beasts of burden sent to do a job, nothing else.

What Egypt didn't reckon for was that God was listening to the children of Israel. Read the first fifteen chapters of Exodus and you'll see the mighty hand of God at work as He softens a harsh slave master and secures freedom for His people.

Moses knew the desert and how to survive in it. He had fled Egypt forty years earlier and had been tending sheep for his father-in-law, Jethro, ever since. Therefore, he knew some of the challenges that would be faced by this newly birthed nation, though not all.

However, God had given Moses a promise:

> And Moses said unto God, Who *am* I, that I should go unto Pharaoh, and that I should bring forth the children of Israel out of Egypt?
> <u>And he said, Certainly I will be with thee; and this</u> <u>*shall be* a token unto thee, that I have sent thee: When</u> <u>thou hast brought forth the people out of Egypt, ye</u> <u>shall serve God upon this mountain.</u>
> (Exodus 3:11-12)

When God promised Moses that He would be with him, God

meant it. The numerous miracles and signs that accompanied the people as they came out of Egypt and lived in the wilderness proved God's Word.

Though the slaves had been brought out of Egypt, slavery still had to be taken out of the people. God accomplished this by faithfully standing by His Word and fulfilling His promises.

Trust Leads To Love

The longer the Israelites were with God, the more they learned they could trust Him. Though they were afraid of God (Exodus 20:18-19), they learned to love and revere Him. The more they loved Him, the less afraid they became. Their love for God drove out their fear. Not only did the Israelites' trust and love drive out fear, but their faith was strengthened as well.

Trust leads to love, which then leads to faith. Faith, then, overcomes fear. This is true because love is such an integral part of faith. The Bible declares that, "perfect love casteth out all fear." Perfect love and faith cannot be separated – they are integral to each other. When love is present and faith is exercised, things happen.

We've seen that Firstfruit giving is different than tithing and other offerings. Tithing and other offerings honor what God has already done, whereas firstfruits honor what God is going to do! Remember, giving firstfruits is prophetically declaring the remainder of the harvest.

Paul declared this principle in Romans, "For if the firstfruit *be* holy, the lump *is* also *holy*: and if the root *be* holy, so *are* the branches" (Rom. 11:16). Prophetic giving is the highest level of giving possible. When you give your firstfruits offering, you make a prophetic declaration that the balance is holy!

This declaration is given out of trust, love and reverence to God. Your faith in God enables you to give firstfruits. If you have faith in the lottery and trust in the world, and decide to give the first part of your raise to a lottery ticket vender, you are gambling on what the world can give. However, giving firstfruits out of faith to God and love for Him is a declaration that your future is secure in Him!

Stepping Out On God's Train

When you place your future in God's hands, you've made a decision that affects every aspect of your life. Giving God your all (and I mean your ALL), means relinquishing control to Him and leaving it there. No more taking hold of the wheel and trying to make something happen.

If you buy a ticket for a train ride, you must get on, find a seat and sit down. You can move around some, but are limited to the cars reserved for passengers. The engineer sits forward in the engine and directs the train. He controls how fast it will go, when it will stop and where it will stop. Your opinion about the control of the train means little to the engineer – he or she is in charge and is doing what they're supposed to do.

Likewise when you step into God's train. When the Holy Ghost cries out "All aboard!" and you find your place, you can rest assured that He won't be coming back to ask you to drive.

Understanding that God has your best interest at heart is paramount to freely giving your firstfruits. God's desire is for you to live in blessing, not curse. God freely bestows blessing as you turn over your life to Him, and leave it there.

Experience with God and His goodness removes all doubt about His intentions for your well-being. Faith overcomes the fear of turning it all over to Him.

Five Steps To Firstfruits Trusting

Step #1: Declare God as your Source.

It's already been determined that God is the source of everything that exists both on the earth and in the universe. Therefore, everything you need is found in God. Declare today that God is your source, not your...

- Job
- Family
- Employer
- Inheritance
- Skills
- Talents
- Intelligence
- Personality

Everything that we see is temporary and ever changing but God who we do not see is eternal and never changes. He was good from the beginning and is yet good today. Your source should be some one who is omnipresent, omniscient, omnipotent, immutable, unquestionable in integrity, unable to lie; cheat; still; who loves you more than you could ever love yourself, and loves you more than any else could ever love you. In all of existence there is only one being that fits the bill. God.

Step #2: Turn over all you have and are to God as your source.

Now that you've made the declaration that God is your source, you must relinquish control of all you have and are to Him. Do you believe that God has your best interest at heart? If not, read this Scripture and see if it changes your mind:

> Ask, and it shall be given you; seek, and ye shall find; knock, and it shall be opened unto you:
>
> For every one that asketh receiveth; and he that seeketh findeth; and to him that knocketh it shall be opened.
>
> Or what man is there of you, whom if his son ask bread, will he give him a stone?
>
> Or if he ask a fish, will he give him a serpent?
>
> If ye then, being evil, know how to give good gifts unto your children, how much more shall your Father which is in heaven give good things to them that ask him?
> (Matt. 7:7-11)

Step #3: Believe God for all your sustenance, not just spiritual things.

When Adam was created, God placed him in a garden that was complete and lacked nothing. Everything was there for Adam's sustenance, including something to do – tend and keep the garden.

God's desire for you is to look to Him for all your needs. Yes. You've been given a brain and many gifts and talents. However, when God energizes your thoughts and quickens your gifts and talents, your efforts are maximized.

The apostle John knew this and expressed it in 3 John 1:2, "Beloved, I wish above all things that thou mayest prosper and be in health, even as thy soul prospereth." When your soul prospers, it's because Jesus has brought you out of the kingdom of darkness into the Kingdom of His glorious light; You renew your mind to the word of God or God's way of doing things (Romans 12:1-3); and as you work the word the Holy spirit aids you.

Then, as you prove God according to His promises (Mal. 3:10), you will see a difference in all that you do. The Bible declares that fear of the Lord is the beginning of wisdom, (Prov. 9:10). Therefore, as you pursue God and His word, your mind will be quickened and you will be given creative ideas. What was once impossible becomes possible.

All this is from God, your Source of life and sustenance.

Step #4: Decide each day to live in Him – choose blessing and life.

Scripture declares that each day you have a choice of how to live. Depending on the choice you make, you'll either live in blessing or in curse:

> Behold, I set before you this day a blessing and a
> curse; A blessing, if ye obey the commandments of
> the LORD your God, which I command you this day:
> And a curse, if ye will not obey the commandments
> of the LORD your God...
> (Deut 11:26-28)

When God sets a decision like this before you, He does it to see if you will follow, His way or yours. By choosing to live for Him, the choice for blessing is made and you'll begin to walk in it.

Among the greatest promises in the Bible is that of God's abiding presence. God has declared that He will never leave you nor forsake you (Heb. 13:5). Proof of this is in the fact that His Holy Spirit indwells you. This means that wherever you go and whatever you do, God can and will direct your path (Prov. 16:9).

When God directs your path, you can rest assured that He will lead you into His blessing.

Step #5: Work with God to release His blessing to others around you.

God blesses you to be a blessing to others. One way you demonstrate trust in God is to freely give of what God has given you. This includes giving your firstfruits.

A pastor related this story. A couple in his church gave first fruit although   at the time they were 98,000.00 dollars in debt. Within two weeks of their gift the debt was forgiven. They began rejoicing immensely but this also caused them to be eligible to adopt a fine baby boy. They adopted the child and are grateful for the teaching on first fruit. They are now able to change a child's life forever.

Abundance like this is what enables us to bless others. See, God doesn't bless us so we can hoard it. He blesses us so we can bless others in His name.

Release God's Abundance In Your Life

Firstfruits giving releases the abundance of God in your life. It's really very simple:

- Trust leads to love.
- Love leads to faith.
- Faith leads to obedience.
- Obedience leads to blessing.
- Blessing leads to abundance.

The challenge is yours today. Are you going to live the abundant life?

CHAPTER 4

God's Firstfruits Offering

For unto us a child is born, unto us a son is given: and the government shall be upon his shoulder: and his name shall be called Wonderful, Counselor, The mighty God, The everlasting Father, The Prince of Peace. Of the increase of his government and peace there shall be no end, upon the throne of David, and upon his kingdom, to order it, and to establish it with judgment and with justice from henceforth even for ever. The zeal of the LORD of hosts will perform this. (Isaiah 9:6-7)

The Bible declares that God gave His Son, Jesus, as a ransom or payment for the sins of the world. This truth is central to the faith of Christianity and vital to the salvation of countless souls from the grip of sin and destruction of Hell.

That Jehovah God would give His Son is unlike any other "god" of the world. Many religions claim to have the truth, but none provide a permanent remedy for sin.

Firstlings As Firstfruits

When the teaching of the firstfruits offering was given through Moses to Israel, it was clearly spoken that firstfruits were just that – the first fruits of one's labors whether in flocks, herds or field (Exodus 34:26). The firstfruits are special and are to be esteemed above the rest of the harvest because they represent the promise of God's provision and abundance.

Cain's offering was unacceptable because he brought "of the fruit" of his harvest. Abel's was acceptable because he brought of the firstlings of his flock. Cain made a choice to reserve the first-fruit for himself and God rejected his offering. Abel, on the other hand, chose to give God the best – the firstlings – to honor Him.

God used the unacceptable offering to teach Cain, and us, a valuable truth. "If you do well, will you not be accepted? And if you do not do well, sin lies at the door. And its desire *is* for you, but you should rule over it" (Gen. 4:7 NKJV). With sin so near, our eyes must never stray from God lest we fall as well.

Firstfruits Must Be The Best

The apostle Paul wrote, "But God demonstrates His own love toward us, in that while we were still sinners, Christ died for us" (Rom. 5:8 NKJV). Christ died for the world before the world knew it even needed a Savior. This action taken by God through Jesus Christ paved the way for humanity to be reconciled to unto God.

We've shown that firstfruits are considered the best of the harvest and prophetically declare the rest of the harvest. Likewise, when God gave His Son as a ransom for all, He gave the best and prophetically declared the harvest.

John wrote:

> For God so loved the world, that he gave his <u>only</u> <u>begotten Son</u>, that whosoever believeth in him should not perish, but have everlasting life.
> For God sent not his Son into the world to condemn the world; but that the world through him might be saved.
> (John 3:16-17)

Jesus, God's only Son, was given out of love for all humanity. Realize that Jesus is God's firstfruit. Jesus is God's first Son. If a person is willing to give their best then they are also saying that everything that they have left is also available to you. Mrs. baker stated it this way in her song "I'm giving you the best that I got "; and then she says "I bet every on my wedding ring, I'm giving you the best that I got". (I thought you would like that). We have similar words in the scriptures; " ³²He that spared not his own Son, but delivered him up for us all, how shall he not with him also freely give us all things?" That's why giving first fruits which is the best is so important. When you refuse to give God your best (first fruit) then you are also telling him that there are other things in your life that you will with hold from Him.

This important truth must be emphasized. God isn't telling us to do anything more than He's already done. He gave His firstfruits, now we give our firstfruits. He gave His best, now we give our best.

Jesus The Son of God

How do we know that Jesus is indeed the Son of God? To answer that question, let's look at some ancient prophecies and accounts of His birth, life, death and resurrection.

There was a prophecy about Jesus in the Garden of Eden. After Adam and Eve ate of the forbidden fruit, God pronounced a judgment upon the serpent that deceived Eve:

> And the LORD God said unto the serpent, Because thou hast done this, thou *art* cursed above all cattle, and above every beast of the field; upon thy belly shalt thou go, and dust shalt thou eat all the days of thy life: <u>And I will put enmity between thee and the woman, and between thy seed and **her seed**; it shall bruise thy head, and thou shalt bruise his heel</u>.
> (Gen. 3:14-15)

> But when the fullness of the time was come, God sent forth his Son, **made of a woman,** made under the law...
> (Gal. 4:4)

That the Lord would come through Judah was prophesied numerous times, including:

> The scepter shall not depart from Judah, nor a lawgiver from between his feet, until Shiloh come; and unto him *shall* the gathering of the people *be*.
> (Gen. 49:10)

For *it is* evident that our Lord sprang out of Juda; of

which tribe Moses spake nothing concerning priest-
hood.
(Heb. 7:14)

Prophecy declared that the Eternal Lord would be born in
Bethlehem:

But thou, Bethlehem Ephratah, *though* thou be little
among the thousands of Judah, *yet* out of thee shall
he come forth unto me *that is* to be ruler in Israel;
whose goings forth *have been* from of old, from
everlasting.
(Micah 5:2)

Now when Jesus was born in Bethlehem of Judaea in
the days of Herod the king, behold, there came wise
men from the east to Jerusalem...
(Matt. 2:1)

Jesus said unto them, Verily, verily, I say unto you,
Before Abraham was, I am.
(John 8:58)

Jesus, the Son of God, would be born of a virgin:

Therefore the Lord himself shall give you a sign;
Behold, **a virgin shall conceive,** and bear a son, and
shall call his name Immanuel.
(Isaiah 7:14)

Now the birth of Jesus Christ was on this wise:
When as his mother Mary was espoused to Joseph,

before they came together, she was found with child of the Holy Ghost.
(Matt. 1:18)

Jesus is the Son of God:
I will declare the decree: the LORD hath said unto me, **Thou *art* my Son;** this day have I begotten thee.
(Psalms 2:7)

And lo a voice from heaven, saying, **this is my beloved Son**, in whom I am well pleased.
(Matt. 3:17)

Jesus, the Son of God, would be executed with other prisoners:
Therefore will I divide him *a portion* with the great, and he shall divide the spoil with the strong; because he hath poured out his soul unto death: and he was numbered with the transgressors; and he bare the sin of many, and made intercession for the transgressors.
(Isaiah 53:12)

And with him they crucify two thieves; the one on his right hand, and the other on his left.
(Mark 15:27)

The Son of God will be resurrected from the grave:
For thou wilt not leave my soul in hell; neither wilt thou suffer thine Holy One to see corruption.
(Psalms 16:10)

And he saith unto them, be not affrighted: Ye seek Jesus of Nazareth, which was crucified: he is risen; he is not here: behold the place where they laid him. (Mark 16:6)

So then after the Lord had spoken unto them, he was received up into heaven, and sat on the right hand of God. (Mark 16:19)

These Scriptures represent only a fraction of what is prophesied about Jesus Christ. However, from this small sampling, you can determine that something about Jesus of Nazareth set Him apart from any other man who ever lived. Not only did the prophets foretell His birth, life, death and resurrection, but all of history has been marked by the life of this one man. No other human being that has ever lived has impacted the world like Jesus.

The Firstfruits of God

Since God offered His Son, Jesus, as His firstfruits offering, some exciting promises have become available. Paul wrote in Romans 11:16, "For if the firstfruit *be* holy, the lump *is* also *holy*: and if the root *be* holy, so *are* the branches." We know that because Jesus is the Son of God that, as firstfruits, He is holy. Therefore, as we are found in Him through our confession of faith, we, the lump, are declared holy as well!

God's declaration of our holiness comes not from what we've done or how good we are, but through the finished work of Jesus on the cross at Calvary. Paul wrote: "Therefore if any man *be* in Christ, *he is* a new creature: old things are passed away; behold, all things are become new" (2 Cor. 5:17). Our status as a new creature is secured through Jesus and His standing as the firstfruits of God. This truth of redemption places us back into the Paradise of God, thus making our election sure.

Gifts Fit For A King

When Jesus was born in Bethlehem, kings traveled from afar to see Him bringing gifts of gold, frankincense, and myrrh. Each category of gifts represented a different aspect of Jesus' position and authority as King, Savior and Lord.

Kings brought gifts to the King. Though Israel didn't recognize their day of salvation, kings from afar did and brought gifts fit for a King. This investment of gold, frankincense and myrrh became part of the wealth of the family in which Jesus was raised. Take hold of this, now, because it shatters the myth that Jesus' family was poor and He was just some out-of-the-way carpenter.

When God offered Jesus as firstfruits, blessing followed Jesus as well. The first verse of Deuteronomy 28 declares the blessings that follow if the person obeys the commandments of God. Jesus is the only person to ever keep the Law, so it naturally follows that He would be subject to the blessings detailed from verse 2 through verse 14. Remember, if the firstfruit is holy, the lump is holy!

Set Apart And Dedicated To The Lord

Jesus was circumcised when He was 8 days old in obedience to the covenant God made with Abram. Recognition of Jesus' divinity came through two unlikely sources, an old prophetess named, Anna, and an old man named Simeon. Both had been waiting in prayer for the Messiah to come, so God allowed both to see Jesus.

According to Paul, Jesus, as Messiah, was the firstborn of many brethren (Rom. 8:29). Being the firstfruits of God meant that others would follow Jesus in His Kingdom. He is our elder brother and the One to whom we look to for salvation.

Jesus was set apart and dedicated to the Lord through the rites of an ancient covenant. We are set apart and dedicated to the Lord through the blood of the New Covenant, Jesus Christ. Jesus was blessed in all that He said and did. Therefore, because we are in Him, the same blessings Jesus was eligible for, are ours as well. We are being molded into His image and likeness. This means that whatever Jesus had, we too can have.

Walk In The Blessing of Firstfruits

Jesus walked in the blessing, so can you. God's promise of blessing belongs just as much to you as it did to Jesus. Why? Because Jesus is your elder brother. You are being molded into the image and likeness of Jesus. Your feet are set on a higher plane. You are seated in heavenly places with Him. You are one of the Kings and Priests of glory. You have the resources of Heaven available to you.

You may wonder how to appropriate the promises of Heaven.

This comes through obedience and devotion to the Lord. Remember in the last chapter we discussed the chain of blessing:

- Trust leads to love.
- Love leads to faith.
- Faith leads to obedience.
- Obedience leads to blessing.
- Blessing leads to abundance.

Walking in the blessing means leaving your will behind and putting on Christ. We'll discuss more aspects of the blessing later in this book, but understand for now that it's far more than stuff – cars, houses, airplanes, money, jewelry, etc. The blessing can best be described as the favor of the Lord that empowers or enables you to prosper in every area of your life.

As you live out your obedience to God through firstfruits giving, you're setting yourself up to receive more than you can possibly imagine. You will prosper in ways you don't now understand because they are beyond your experience. However, God will bring you there.

Take hold of Jesus today. As you do, He will lead you through the power of the Holy Spirit to levels of faith and giving that you cannot even fathom today. All as you prophesy your future through firstfruits giving.

CHAPTER 5

The Firstfruits of Self

*I beseech you therefore, brethren, by the mercies of
God, that ye present your bodies a living sacrifice,
holy, acceptable unto God, which is your reasonable
service.*

*And be not conformed to this world: but be ye trans-
formed by the renewing of your mind, that ye may
prove what is that good, and acceptable, and perfect,
will of God.*

(Romans 12:1-2)

Firstfruits must be the best. In Numbers 18:12 God instructs the
children of Israel to give first fruits and that it must be the
best… "All the best of the oil, and all the best of the wine, and of
the wheat, the firstfruits of them which they shall offer unto the
LORD, them have I given thee. We discovered in the last chapter
that God offered firstfruits as well, and that His offering was the
very best, His own Son, Jesus.

This chapter will examine the firstfruits of self. What does it
mean to offer yourself as firstfruits unto God? How do you offer

your body a living sacrifice as the Scripture above commands? It's one thing to offer something to God that you have obtained, quite another to offer yourself.

Jesus Christ – The Holy One of God

Firstfruits giving is prophetic. Therefore, above all others, firstfruits offerings must be set apart as holy unto God. Anything less and the offering is tainted and unacceptable.

Jesus declared, "If any *man* will come after me, let him deny himself, and take up his cross, and follow me" (Matt. 16:24). Jesus' proclamation firmly established the righteous nature of giving oneself to God. Furthermore, the act of taking up one's cross only leads to one place – Golgotha, the place of sacrifice.

That Jesus was, and is, holy is beyond dispute. His holiness far exceeds that of any man who ever lived or ever will live. We know that Jesus is God because of the testimony of Scripture and the confirming witness of the Holy Spirit. "For I *am* the LORD your God: ye shall therefore sanctify yourselves, and ye shall be holy; for I *am* holy" (Lev. 11:44).

Holy In The Lord Jesus Christ

Paul wrote in Romans 11:16, "For if the firstfruit *be* holy, the lump *is* also *holy*: and if the root *be* holy, so *are* the branches." Jesus Christ is the firstfruit of God and He is holy. Therefore, if you are in Christ, then you, as the lump, are also holy. Jesus is the root and you are the branch. If He is the root and the root is holy, then as a branch off that root, you are holy as well.

Understand this: We as a believers are holy because of Christ, not because of what we have done. We cannot earn or aspire to holiness. It is bestowed upon us as part of the divine exchange. It's part of the free gift of salvation.

Therefore, because holiness is appointed to us according to our position in Christ Jesus, we have got nothing to boast about. Furthermore, our salvation is no by works. The scriptures put it this way…. [8]For by grace are ye saved through faith; and that not of yourselves: *it is* the gift of God: [9]Not of works, lest any man should boast…(Ephesians 2:8-9).

Paul declared, "Therefore if any man *be* in Christ, *he is* a new creature: old things are passed away; behold, all things are become new" (2 Cor. 5:17). So what is it that becomes new? Everything! God doesn't just take your old sinful man and put new clothes on him to spark him up some. God gives you a new identity in Him that far surpasses anything you ever had before. The key is being in Christ.

Therefore, if you're a new creation, why do some Christians still…

- Use the same old filthy language?
- Wallow around in unbelief?
- Watch the same trash on TV or at the movies?
- Listen jokes that are below your character?
- Refuse to give God what is rightfully His?

Firstfruits of Your Mind

If you've lived on this planet and been subject to any of the lies of the enemy, your mind is tainted and must be renewed. Everyone begins life on earth the same way – a tiny egg quickened by an even tinier sperm. Fertilization methods may vary due to modern marvels of science, but it all comes down to the sperm and egg coming together.

Almost immediately, the baby growing inside is subjected to the lies of the enemy. Wherever the mother goes, the baby goes as well. What the mother listens to, the baby hears. The food the mother eats nourishes the baby. If the mother uses drugs the baby gets addicted and on and on and on.

When the baby is born, the senses are fully aware and the infant begins to grow. Surrounded by the world, the messages of the enemy are drilled into the mind of this innocent little one, seeking to gain a foothold of destruction to be capitalized on later in life. Messages like, "You're…

- Too small."
- Too big."
- Stupid."
- A girl."
- A boy."
- Too fat."
- Too skinny."
- Black."
- White."
- Poor."
- Rich."
- Too religious."
- Not religious enough."

You get the point.

The only way to escape the mindset of the world is to replace it with a Heavenly mindset, "Let this mind be in you, which was also in Christ Jesus…" (Phil. 2:5). The promise of the gospel of Christ is that you can and will be changed – you don't have to stay the way you are.

Part of the process of renewing your mind is filling it with the truth of God and His promises. You must replace the lies of the enemy with truth from God's word and demolish the strongholds in your mind with the power of the Holy Ghost. Paul wrote that we must cast down Imaginations (mental pictures) and also every high thing that exalts itself against the knowledge of God and bring into captivity every thought to the obedience of Christ. (2nd Corinthians 10:5).

> My son, forget not my law; but let thine heart keep my commandments:
> For length of days, and long life, and peace, shall they add to thee.
> Let not mercy and truth forsake thee: bind them about thy neck; write them upon the table of thine heart:
> So shalt thou find favor and good understanding in the sight of God and man.
> Trust in the LORD with all thine heart; and lean not unto thine own understanding.
> In all thy ways acknowledge him, and he shall direct thy paths.
> Be not wise in thine own eyes: fear the LORD, and depart from evil.
> It shall be health to thy navel, and marrow to thy bones.

Honor the LORD with thy substance, and with the firstfruits of all thine increase:
So shall thy barns be filled with plenty, and thy presses shall burst out with new wine.
(Prov. 3:1-10)

Offer Your Body...

Offering your body to Jesus as a living sacrifice declares to both Him and you that you are serious in your walk. Have you ever noticed that cheapskates talk a lot about what they do and how much they know? Well, talk is cheap, but the walk will cost you something.

Have you submitted every member of your body to God? You know what I mean. Your tongue, your eyes, and ears, hands and feet, your sexual organs? See. By offering all your members to God so that Jesus may be glorified in your body, God is released to do in you what He wants done.

Paul talked about the war that goes on inside us in Galatians 5:17-23. He writes that the Spirit wars against the flesh and the flesh against the Spirit. He lists what the works of the flesh are, including, "Adultery, fornication, uncleanness, lasciviousness, Idolatry, witchcraft, hatred, variance, emulations, wrath, strife, seditions, heresies, Envyings, murders, drunkenness, revellings, and such like" (Gal. 5:19-21).

Then Paul goes on to discuss what happens when we are filled with the Holy Spirit of God. "But the fruit of the Spirit is love, joy, peace, longsuffering, gentleness, goodness, faith, Meekness, [and] temperance" (Gal 5:22-23).

How does one change from being a drunken, murderous, idolatrous, unclean reveler? "And they that are Christ's have <u>crucified the flesh</u> with the affections and lusts" (Gal 5:24).

This is what it means to "take up your cross" and follow Jesus: You deny the desires of your flesh, offer every member of your body to God for Him to do with as He pleases, set your eyes on Christ and the high calling He has on your life, and you follow Him. Yes you are not a mistake; no matter how you got here. God has a calling (plan and a purpose) for your life.

Your Mind Renewed

By setting your thoughts, actions, and attention on Jesus and the calling on your life as one of His, you automatically begin to undergo a change of mind. Suddenly, what was important is not important any more. You find yourself unable to do the same things with the same people like before. Your thoughts are on God and not the world or yourself.

Renewal of your mind comes as you immerse yourself in Christ. You become more and more accustomed to being in Him and find that when you slip, you cannot tolerate a moment without His presence. You embark on a life of repentance.

Repentance is the act of recognizing wrong decisions, wrong actions or wrong direction, and changing. To repent is to change direction and go another way. The Holy Spirit leads you to repentance through kindness. (Romans 2:4) God never condemns us. A perfect example of this the story of the woman caught in the act of adultery (John 8:3-11) Jesus said to this woman ...Woman, where are those thine accusers? hath no man condemned thee? [11] She said,

No man, Lord. And Jesus said unto her, neither do I condemn thee: go, and sin no more. God's attitude is to forgive you not to condemn you. Once you have repented and confessed that sin unto God he is faithful and just to forgive you of that sin and to cleans you from all unrighteousness (1st John 1:9). Then you must refuse to walk under condemnation. Romans 8:1 states...[1]*There is* therefore now no condemnation to them which are in Christ Jesus, who walk not after the flesh, but after the Spirit.

The enemy will do his best to heap guilt and shame on you through condemnation to fill you with remorse. However, remorse doesn't lead anywhere except self-destruction.

The Firstfruits of Self

God desires the best from you. He gave His best; now give Him your best. This entire chapter has been devoted to helping you understand how to be a clean, holy, firstfruit offering unto God. But now it's up to you. You are the only one who can determine when, where and how much to give to God.

What does it mean to be totally sold-out to God?

It means living your life in such a way that people know you are not of this world.

When Jesus was crucified, a Roman soldier was attending at the foot of the cross. When Jesus cried out and gave up His Spirit, the soldier declared, "Certainly this was a righteous man" (Luke 23:47).

What would someone who didn't know you say in a similar circumstance? Would they be able to tell that your life was different because of what the Lord Jesus had done in and through you?

We live in a convenience society: Fast food, express lanes, drive-through banking and church on TV. However, living the Christian life is not convenient. In fact, it's often downright inconvenient. The demand of righteousness means we live to a higher standard and march to a different drummer. Our call is heavenward, not earthbound.

God wants your best. Give it to Him.

Remember, firstfruits giving is prophetic. Therefore, as you prophetically give your firstfruits best to Him, your entire life will be blessed: "For if the firstfruit *be* holy, the lump *is* also *holy*" (Romans 11:16).

Walk out your salvation by giving yourself a living sacrifice to God. Move in the realm of holiness that God has called you into. Take hold of the promise that He will never leave you nor forsake you and press in to Him.

I assure you, that as you do the blessing of God will rest on you. What's the blessing? Keep on reading and you'll discover another realm of living that far exceeds anything you've experienced till now.

CHAPTER 6

The Power in your Hands.

*...that he (the priest) may cause the blessing to rest
in thy house.*
(Ezekiel 44:30)

*For if the firstfruit be holy, the lump is also holy: and
if the root be holy, so are the branches.*
(Romans 11:16)

*Is the seed yet in the barn? yea, as yet the vine, and
the fig tree, and the pomegranate, and the olive tree,
hath not brought forth: from this day will I bless you.*
(Hag. 2: 19)

God's promises are sure and will be fulfilled. Scripture is filled with instance after instance where the Word of God was accomplished as declared by the mouth of two or three witnesses. The prophet Isaiah declared: "For as the rain cometh down, and the snow from heaven, and returneth not thither, but watereth the earth, and maketh it bring forth and bud, that it may give seed to the sower, and bread to the eater: So shall my word be that goeth forth out of my mouth: it shall not return unto me void, but it shall accomplish that which I please, and it shall prosper *in the thing* whereto I sent it" (Isaiah 55:10-11).

Throughout this book the promises of God are examined to establish His Word, not mine or any other man's. It matters less what a man says than what God says. If God says so, God will bring it forth. If a man says so, it's up to that man to bring it to pass.

The teaching contained in the last two chapters is vital to the proper understanding of God's Word in this chapter. To receive God's blessing, you must first realize through Whom – Jesus – it comes. To prosper in God's blessing, you must find your place in Him through Christ and offer yourself as firstfruits as well.

There is a difference between receiving God's blessing and prospering in God's blessing. For many, receiving it is enough; they're happy dabbling in the "stuff" of the blessing. However, for others, it's prospering in the blessing; it's not all about the stuff.

What The Blessing Is Not

Christians for many years have mistakenly understood the bless-ing of God to be stuff – cars, houses, airplanes, jewels, gold, money, etc. These can be signs or symptoms that the blessing has indeed landed but they are not the blessing. For instance, no one is going to Hell for the effects of the Sin Nature i.e. Smoking; Drinking; Cursing; Committing Adultery; Pre-marital sex; Lying; Cheating; Stealing; ..ect. No if one goes to hell it will be because their Sin Nature has not been exchanged with the Nature of God. Yet people are called sinners because the effects of the Sin Nature that can be seen in their lives. Actually you don't really see the sin nature that lives within a person. Another of way of saying it; I as a husband take my wife out on a date every week, I open the car door for her, send her roses "just because", and most times whenever we part even if I am just leaving the table in a restaurant I kiss her. In fact once when we were on a cruise ship in Hawaii on our fourth anniversary, I got up from the table to go to the restroom. After walking about eight feet from the table I remembered that I had not kissed my wife. So I turned around and went back to the table. The eyes of every one became fixed on me to see what I was doing. I leaned over and kissed my spouse and a lady said look at the love he has for his wife. Well, all these actions are not love but they are the effects of the over-whelming love that I have for my wife. The stuff can be the effects of the blessing but not necessarily the Blessing.

The blessing of God is far more than stuff. Remember, God created everything. Why would He limit His blessing to just the abundance of things? It's time we revisit the meaning of the blessing of God and discover what it really means.

What The Blessing Is

God's blessing is visibly manifested in many ways, including, success in the marketplace, financial freedom and possessions like automobiles, houses, gold jewelry, etc. However, as already stated, when given by God, these are not the blessing, only a visible manifestation of the blessing.

God's blessing can also be described as God's favor. When one operates under the favor of God, nothing stands in the way that cannot be moved. The blessing is an empowerment, A Divine enablement, A God rubbed on ability. That's right, the Blessing is the Anointing. It will cause you to prosper and be successful in every area of your life. When you give firstfruits the bible states that the priest once he dedicates it to the Lord, will cause the blessing to rest in your house. Let's look at a few examples of the awesome power that is released when someone gives (sows) it.

First fruit Giving

In Exodus chapters 11 and 12 we see the awesome power of first fruit giving. The children of Israel have been in slavery for 400 years. God sends them a deliverer whose name was Moses. Moses says to their captor Pharaoh" God said let my people go". Pharaoh refuses and 9 plagues ensue. But Pharaoh still wants to keep God's people enslaved. Now the power of firstfruits becomes a factor. God instructs the children of Israel to have each household take a part in sacrificing a lamb or goat. Barbecuing it but putting the blood on the doorpost. Why? Because the death angle was coming (the 10th plague) to take all first born of man or beast that wasn't dedicated to God as firstfruits. At the time some Israelites might not have known that sacrificing the lamb or goat was actually causing their firstborns to be redeemed. But God knew. When the death angle came that night the firstborn of the Egyptians whether of man or beast died. But the firstborn of the Israelites and their beast lived. After four hundred years of slavery in one knight the slaves were set free. Pharaoh said you and your people with all their possessions are free to go. The awesome power of firstfruits giving caused at least 3million slaves to be set free in one day. Not only were they released but also they came out of slavery rich, and healed. Exodus 13:1-16, psalm 105:37.

Let's look at another type of firstfruits giving. In 1st Kings we have the story of a prophet of God being to sent to a widow woman during the time of a three-year draught. Elisha went to the city Zarephath and saw this widow women gathering sticks. He asks her to bring him a little container of water and as she was going to get it Elisha also ask for a piece of bread. She then says "¹² But she said, "I swear by the Lord your God that I don't have a single piece of bread in the house. And I have only a handful of flour left in the jar and a little cooking oil in the bottom of the jug. I was just gathering a few sticks to cook this last meal, and then my son and I were going to eat it and die". Then the prophet utter words that wouldn't be politically correct today. Make me some cake **first** and bring it to me. The nerve of that preacher taking bread out of the mouth of a widower and her son. Well she made God's representative a little cake first and from that day until the water draught was over neither her flour nor oil ran out. No matter how much she used there was always some left. That's awesome power!

Then there is Joseph another type of firstfruit. He was the first born son of Rachel. Although he was despised by his brothers, this man had the favor or blessing of God on him.

He was sown by God... *And it came to pass, when Joseph was come unto his brethren, that they stript Joseph out of his coat, his coat of many colours that was on him; And they took him, and cast him into a pit: and the pit was empty, there was no water in it.* Genesis 37:23-24. Then became a slave... *¹And Joseph was brought down to Egypt; and Potiphar, an officer of Pharaoh, captain of the guard, an Egyptian, bought him of the hands of the Ishmeelites, which had brought him down thither.* Genesis 39:1. Yet even being a slave could not stop the blessing that was on this first-fruit, the slave named Joseph. Look at this report of this slave ... *And the LORD was with Joseph, and he was a prosperous man; and he was in the house of his master the Egyptian..* As if being a slave wasn't bad enough, next Joseph was put into prison. Lets see what the report will be about this incarcerated man who appears by all accounts so far that the favor of God is on him... *Then Joseph's master took him and put him into the prison, a place where the king's prisoners were confined. And he was there in the prison.* [21] *But the Lord was with Joseph and showed him mercy, and He gave him favor in the sight of the keeper of the prison.* [22] *And the keeper of the prison committed to Joseph's hand all the prisoners who were in the prison; whatever they did there, it was his doing.* [23] *The keeper of the prison did not look into anything that was under Joseph's authority, because the Lord was with him; and whatever he did, the Lord made it prosper.* Wow Look what happens when the blessing is on an individual. You will do well to remember this. No matter what has been taken from you, or what you seem to have lost, know that if the blessing is resting on your life greater will be restored. Remember Joseph coat of many colors that his brothers took from him and ripped it up? Well, look what happened next. *Then Pharaoh took his signet ring off his hand and put it on Joseph's hand; and he clothed him in garments of fine linen and put a gold chain around his neck.* (Genesis 41:42) From the dungeon to the palace because the blessing was on him. Praise God!!!

Note: Genesis 45:5 God sowed first fruit (Joseph).

In Genesis the 22nd Chapter Father Abraham gave first fruit (Isaac) and God said because Abraham did this; in blessing I will bless you and in multiplying I will multiply your seed as the stars of the heavens and the sand of the sea shore, and your seed will possess the gate of their enemies; and in your seed shall all the nations of the earth be blessed. Now today there are those who don't believe in the hundred-fold return but look at what father Abraham has received after giving first fruit. All the millions of people who by faith have accepted Jesus as their Lord and Savior are part of Abraham's seed. Incidentally that is more than one hundred fold return.

For God so loved the world that He gave FirstFruit (Jesus); His best. Talk about awesome power of firstfruits giving, lets count God's harvest. Lest start off with the number of people the John gave witness to in the book of revelation. This number according to Revelation 7:9 is innumerable. If a firstfruits is important enough for God to give, it must be important to God for believers to partake in this higher level of giving.

The Blessing is for many Reasons.

God blesses His people for many reasons, including:

1. God blesses out of His infinite love and mercy to ensure that all our needs and wants are met. "But my God shall supply all your need according to his riches in glory by Christ Jesus" (Phil. 4:19). Delight thyself also in the LORD; and he shall give thee the desires of thine heart. (Psalms 37:4)

2. God blesses His people so they will become conduits of His blessing for others.
   > And <u>all people of the earth shall see that thou art called by the name of the LORD</u>…
   > And the LORD shall make thee plenteous in goods, in the fruit of thy body, and in the fruit of thy cattle, and in the fruit of thy ground, in the

land which the LORD sware unto thy fathers to give thee.

The LORD shall open unto thee his good treasure, the heaven to give the rain unto thy land in his season, and to bless all the work of thine hand: and <u>thou shalt lend unto many nations, and thou shalt not borrow</u>. (Deut. 28:10-12)

[1]Now the LORD had said unto Abram, Get thee out of thy country, and from thy kindred, and from thy father's house, unto a land that I will shew thee: [2]And I will make of thee a great nation, and I will bless thee, and make thy name great; and thou shalt be a blessing: [3]And I will bless them that bless thee, and curse him that curseth thee: and in thee shall all families of the earth be blessed. (Genesis 12:1-3)

3. God's blessing releases resources on the earth to bring about His Kingdom. "In that I command thee this day to love the LORD thy God, to walk in his ways, and to keep his commandments and his statutes and his judgments, that thou mayest live and multiply: and <u>the LORD thy God shall bless thee in the land whither thou goest to possess it</u>" (Deut. 30:16).

When the blessing is bestowed on you, things begin to change. What once seemed impossible suddenly becomes possible because God's favor kicks in.

Sowing Out of Love

One of David's most reverent acts of worship was the offering he made to God for the Temple that Solomon would eventually build. Not only did he seek to honor God by building the Temple, but he also honored God through this prophetic, firstfruits offering.

David didn't consider his possessions something to keep and hoard, but considered all that he owned a result of God's blessing. Therefore, "David prepared abundantly before his death" (1 Chron. 22:5). Let's look at the preparations David made to have the Temple built:

- 100,000 talents of gold – about 3,750 tons – $37,511,450,000 at today's value
- 1,000,000 talents of silver – about 37,500 tons – $552,000,000 at today's value
- quantities of bronze and iron to great to weigh – invaluable
- great quantities of wood and stone – invaluable

The value of just the silver and gold is more than 38 billion dollars! Imagine the pounding in David's heart as he committed this treasure trove unto the Lord for something to be built after he was dead!

All of his life, David sowed out of his love for the Lord. Love-motivated giving moved David into the realm of sowing for the harvest. Likewise, love must motivate us as we give. Anything less, and we're giving for the wrong reasons. Remember, God looks at the heart to understand what the hand is doing (1 Sam. 16:7).

Sowing For The Blessing

As you prepare to sow firstfruits offerings, make ready your heart. The Bible declares that, "The heart *is* deceitful above all *things*, and desperately wicked" (Jer. 17:9). Therefore, examine your heart and get it right with God.

Sowing for the blessing requires a pure heart. Cain's heart was darkened toward God and his offering was rejected. Likewise, Ananias and Sapphira came before the Lord with deceitful hearts and were stricken dead. Purify your heart and come openly before the Lord. The promise given to Cain is just as valid today as it was thousands of years ago: "If thou doest well, shalt thou not be accepted?" (Gen. 4:7).

You may not have 38 billion dollars to give as a firstfruits offering, but you have something. You decide in your heart what to give – there is no prescribed amount. Paul declared, "Every man according as he purposeth in his heart, *so let him give*; not grudgingly, or of necessity: for God loveth a cheerful giver" (2 Cor. 9:7). See the importance of the heart? You give according to what you purpose in it.

Are You Ready?

Jesus was standing adjacent to the Temple treasury watching people cast in their offerings. For some, it was a big show – one coin clanging into the treasury at a time. For others, it was drudgery. However, for one poor widow, it was an act of worship:

> And he looked up, and saw the rich men casting
> their gifts into the treasury.

And he saw also a certain poor widow casting in thither two mites.

And he said, Of a truth I say unto you, that this poor widow hath cast in more than they all:

For all these have of their abundance cast in unto the offerings of God: but she of her penury hath cast in all the living that she had.

(Luke 21:1-4)

What's the condition of your heart? Are you ready to step into another realm of giving? Are you prepared to sow for the blessing of God? Are you ready to give it all out of love?

If the answer is "Yes!" then purpose in your heart what your firstfruits offering will be (remember, your firstfruits must be the best). Once you've made that decision, give it to the man or woman of God over your house of worship so he or she can wave it before the Lord and command God's blessing over you. Then, be prepared for God's blessing – His favor – to rest upon you and your household.

CHAPTER 7

Breakthrough Power

⟶⟩•⟨⟵

Thus saith the LORD, the Holy One of Israel, and his Maker, Ask me of things to come…and concerning the work of my hands command ye me.
(Isaiah 45:11)

We've learned that obedience to tithing and giving offerings opens the windows of heaven (Mal. 3:10). We've also discovered that firstfruits offerings are prophetic in nature because firstfruits declare what God <u>will</u> do, while tithes and other offerings praise God for what He has already done.

Another aspect of firstfruits giving is the requirement that firstfruits be the best. God gave His best in Jesus and so He requires our best as well. Whether we give out of our production or the firstfruits of self, give God the best.

This chapter introduces you to the breakthrough power of the firstfruits offering. You'll see how God established this offering so that you, as His child, may declare your future and then walk into it.

Stop Believing The Lie

For centuries, the church has been stuck in a poverty mindset. The history of this can be traced back to the monastic movement in which people were encouraged to take a vow of poverty and separate themselves from all outside influences.

These monks declared that Jesus lived a life of poverty according to the Scriptures and that they should forsake all and do the same. Some even went so far as to say that bathing was an unnecessary luxury and therefore, unholy.

For centuries, men and women of God were forced to live as paupers as "God did His purifying work in them." Even today, we see the effects of this flawed interpretation of Scripture, as many Christians accept poverty as their lot from God.

This poverty mentality carries over into the tithes and offerings of these deceived Christians. Because they are barely getting by; living from paycheck to pay check, they think that giving to God will make them even poorer. They don't view God as a generous, benevolent provider, they view Him as a harsh taskmaster, wanting everything they have and giving nothing.

It's time to stop believing the lie. It's time to gain an understanding of God that transcends money and possessions. It's time to get a heavenly view of God instead of an earthy one.

Positioned For Prosperity

When God placed Adam in the Garden of Eden, He placed him in a lush garden, filled with fruit and plenty. The Garden of Eden was not some half-finished, partially done mess – it was complete and fruitful.

The design was for Adam to tend and keep what was already there, not begin something from nothing and hope it worked out. God is the One who began with nothing – Adam had it all placed before him.

We can see from the account in Genesis 2:11 that God even let Adam know where the "good" gold was. Furthermore, Adam was given dominion over it all – everything God created. He was positioned for prosperity like no other man who ever lived. Adam and Eve were to dominate all living things and within their domain was the wealth of the world.

Knowing that Adam was positioned for prosperity and that God was the One who positioned him so, it's easy to discern that the plan set forth in the Garden is God's plan for humanity. God's desire is for us to prosper as well.

Because of sin, Adam fell from his high estate. God declared that from then on, Adam would have to earn his keep by the sweat of his brow (Gen. 3:17-19).

We still must work; God hasn't taken that requirement away. However, the anointing of God will cause us to have **sweatless victory**

The Promise of Blessing

We've already discussed the blessing that comes through obedience to God. However, it bears repeating – God did not create you to see how little you need to "get by." God created you to be His ambassador (2 Cor. 5:20) on earth. As His ambassador, you represent God, the King of Heaven that created everything in existence.

Therefore, it makes sense that He would equip you to properly present Him to others.

Moses understood this because of his familiarity with the palaces of Egypt. Remember, Moses was in line to be the next pharaoh until he fled into the wilderness.

Moses' upbringing in the palace of the king helped him understand the protocols of royal government. He understood that when the king commissioned a person as an ambassador, they had certain rights and responsibilities conveyed because of that appointment. Furthermore, when they spoke, they spoke with the authority of the king behind them.

However, Moses also understood what happened to these officials if they became corrupt and refused to obey the dictates of the king; they were removed from office and were usually executed. Knowing this makes it easier for you to understand these commands of God delivered through Moses:

> Behold, I set before you this day a blessing and a curse;
> A blessing, if ye obey the commandments of the LORD your God, which I command you this day:
> And a curse, if ye will not obey the commandments of the LORD your God, but turn aside out of the way which I command you this day, to go after other gods, which ye have not known.
> (Deut. 11:26-28)

> And it shall come to pass, if thou shalt hearken diligently unto the voice of the LORD thy God, to observe *and* to do all his commandments which I command thee this day, that the LORD thy God will

set thee on high above all nations of the earth:
And all these blessings shall come on thee, and over-
take thee, if thou shalt hearken unto the voice of the
LORD thy God...
(Deut. 28:1-2)

See, I have set before thee this day life and good,
and death and evil;
In that I command thee this day to love the LORD
thy God, to walk in his ways, and to keep his
commandments and his statutes and his judgments,
that thou mayest live and multiply: and the LORD
thy God shall bless thee in the land whither thou
goest to possess it.
But if thine heart turn away, so that thou wilt not
hear, but shalt be drawn away, and worship other
gods, and serve them;
I denounce unto you this day, that ye shall surely
perish, *and that* ye shall not prolong *your* days upon
the land, whither thou passest over Jordan to go to
possess it.
I call heaven and earth to record this day against
you, *that* I have set before you life and death, blessing and cursing: therefore choose life, that both thou
and thy seed may live...
(Deut. 30:15-19)

Notice in each of these examples that God promised blessing
for obedience and curse for disobedience. Moses was able to understand this because of personal experience and bring it to the people

in a way they could understand.

Commanding Your Own Breakthrough

Many of you are experiencing blessing and breakthrough now because your mama prayed. Others of you are blessed because your grandma and granddad prayed about their seed to come, and you're it. But now, God wants you to take the responsibility for commanding your breakthrough.

You command breakthrough by speaking God's Word. You can't just have it in your heart you've got to speak it as well. This is of primary importance, especially in firstfruits giving. The Bible says that you must make a statement as you sow your firstfruits (Deuteronomy 26:10). This statement is your prophetic utterance of what God will do in and through you.

When you give and declare your firstfruits it honors God. You are conveying to God that you know that it was He who brought you out of the kingdom of darkness, into the kingdom of His dear Son. God has led you from the land of not enough (Egypt), through the land of just enough (the wilderness), to the land of more than enough (the promised land). Therefore, you give unto God, the firstfruit so that the blessing will rest in your house."

By declaring before God, you set in motion the laws of blessing and prosperity. You become like the ambassador who is perfectly representing the king. You begin to walk in favor before God and man like you've never walked before. You begin commanding your own breakthrough!

Submit To The Word of God In You

As God's ambassador, you need not worry about anything. God is the King. He is the One in control. All you need to do is walk in obedience. Then, as you make declarations before God, you make them with the authority of Heaven and witness God's "dunamis" – His miracle working power in your life.

The Bible declares that the Word is near you already: "But the word *is* very nigh unto thee, in thy mouth, and in thy heart, that thou mayest do it" (Deut. 30:14). God puts His Word in your heart and mouth so that you can live it out. Then, when you need it the most, it's already there. Isaiah 55:11 says "So shall my word be that goeth forth out of my mouth: it shall not return unto me void, but it shall accomplish that which I please, and it shall prosper *in the thing* whereto I sent it". When you get God's Word on the inside and then speak it, it will have the same result as if God spoke it. When the Holy Spirit energizes the mighty power of God's Word in you, you become unstoppable.

God gave you His Word for a reason: To live out God's purpose and plan on earth. He gives His Word to accomplish His plan, His way.

Nevertheless, with God's Word in you, you begin to command your own breakthrough. You begin to sow firstfruits and declare God's promises over it to see your harvest come in. The blessing, which is the favor of God, the empowerment of God, the ability to prosper in every area of your life, begins to rest in your house. You then begin experiencing the mighty breakthrough power of first-fruits giving.

Now it going to take some work to get Gods Word securely planted in your heart. You must spend time in it. Get to know God's

Word by devouring it, meditating it, and living it. You must take an active role in placing God's Word in your heart by studying it and making it a part of your life. Then, when you are faced with situations or problems in your life, God's Word that dwells richly in you will rise up as you speak it and bring you the victory you seek. You become bold and confident in God's Word because you know it works. Furthermore, you don't have to wonder what the Word says; you'll know what it says.

Bold As A Lion – Gentle As A Dove

When God's Word rises up in you, boldness rises up as well. Jesus didn't shrink back from anything God desired Him to do. He knew that God's Word was established and would accomplish everything for which it was sent.

Therefore, trust in the Lord and in the Word of God that is in your heart. Don't be afraid of the enemy. Use the Word of God against the devil. It works every time. The Bible says: "Submit yourselves therefore to God. Resist the devil, and he will flee from you. Draw nigh to God, and he will draw nigh to you" (James 4:7-8).

As you put this into practice in your life, you'll begin to see a dramatic change. First, you'll find yourself becoming stronger and stronger in your battle against sin. Then, you'll begin to notice tenderness in your heart toward others as they seek to draw closer into the presence of God. Finally, you'll declare God's Word with no doubt that it will be fulfilled and accomplished.

Live According To God's Word

Giving firstfruits is just the beginning of this incredible journey of holiness. As you give, you'll begin to prophetically declare the promises of God over your life and over your family as well. You'll begin to see lives changed and prophecy fulfilled as you walk with the Lord, in tune with His Spirit and hearing His voice. This is what it means to live according to God's Word.

The further and deeper you go in God means more opportunities for Him to use you to fulfill His plan on earth. You then become a conduit of God's blessing for countless souls in need of His loving touch.

This is the reason for the blessing:
- To empower you to prosper in every area of your life.
- To clothe you with the favor of God
- To enable you to get the job done God's way
- To be a blessing to others

Now that you know the secrets of the breakthrough power of firstfruits giving, what are you going to do with them? Are you willing to put your life on the line and become a conduit of blessing for others? Are you prepared to command your own breakthrough so you can show others how to command theirs?

If you answered yes to these questions, then you are well on the way to walking in a new dimension of God's glory and grace. So, get ready to receive your promise.

CHAPTER 8

Receive Your Promise

*Honour the LORD with thy substance, and with the
firstfruits of all thine increase:
So shall thy barns be filled with plenty, and thy
presses shall burst out with new wine.*
(Prov 3:9-10)

Throughout this book it's been shown that God's desire is to bless you with plenty and success. You've also learned that there are some things necessary for you to do to walk in God's blessing. Of primary importance is the requirement stated in the Scripture above.

Last chapter we discussed the breakthrough power of giving firstfruits offerings. This power comes through the prophetic nature of firstfruits giving and opens the windows of Heaven unlike any other offering.

This chapter will help you understand how to receive the promise of the blessing. Unless you know the promise, how can you receive it, or how can you receive it if you're not ready?

God wants you equipped to receive everything He has for you. Therefore, let go of the past and take hold of the future. He has promised to bless His children with the same blessing He gave to Abraham:

The Promise:
And give thee the blessing of Abraham, to thee, and to thy seed with thee; that thou mayest inherit the land wherein thou art a stranger, which God gave unto Abraham.
(Gen. 28:4).

The Blessing:
Now the LORD had said unto Abram, Get thee out of thy country, and from thy kindred, and from thy father's house, unto a land that I will show thee:
And I will make of thee a great nation, and I will bless thee, and make thy name great; and thou shalt be a blessing:
And I will bless them that bless thee, and curse him that curseth thee: and in thee shall all families of the earth be blessed.
(Gen. 12:1-3)

Let's see what it takes to get the blessing.

God Is Not Out To Get You

Many people think that God is just looking for an excuse to hammer them. They believe that God is waiting for them to slip so

He can come down hard on them and destroy them. Their image of God is that of a harsh, malevolent, taskmaster who wants nothing good for them but everything good for Him.

This twisted view of God usually results from unfulfilled expectations of Him that are unholy. One may want God to do something contrary to His will or Word, and then gets angry at God when He doesn't grant their wish. However, God will not change His Law, His Word, or His way just because someone expects the wrong thing.

This truth is what separates Jehovah God from every other "deity" in the universe. Yahweh, Jehovah, is a God of love and mercy. Scripture affirms His love and concern for mankind and portrays Him as a benevolent creator:

> He that spared not his own Son, but delivered him up
> for us all, how shall he not with him also freely give
> us all things?
> (Rom. 8:32).

> But God commendeth his love toward us, in that,
> while we were yet sinners, Christ died for us.
> (Rom. 5:8)

> For God so loved the world, that he gave his only
> begotten Son, that whosoever believeth in him
> should not perish, but have everlasting life.
> For God sent not his Son into the world to condemn
> the world; but that the world through him might be
> saved.
> (John 3:16-17)

> Beloved, let us love one another: for love is of God;

and every one that loveth is born of God, and knoweth God.

He that loveth not knoweth not God; for God is love.
In this was manifested the love of God toward us,
because that God sent his only begotten Son into the
world, that we might live through him.

Herein is love, not that we loved God, but that he
loved us, and sent his Son *to be* the propitiation for
our sins.

Beloved, if God so loved us, we ought also to love
one another.

(1 John 4:7-11)

Three Keys To Receiving God's Promises

Unlocking God's promises in your life is as simple as one, two,
three. Outlined below are three keys that unlock the windows of
heaven to receive God's promise of blessing.

Key #1: Obedience

When you receive Jesus as your Savior, the next step is to know
Him as Lord. This only happens as you submit your life to Him.
Submission is the act of surrendering your arms of rebellion and
learning to walk arm-in-arm with Jesus. Paul declared, "For as
many as are led by the Spirit of God, they are the sons of God"
(Rom. 8:14).

For the Holy Spirit to lead your life, you must be willing. This
willingness comes as a decision and is supported and bolstered each
day by the same decision – to be led of God.

Jesus lived a life of obedience to the Father and never went anywhere or did anything without the Father leading Him there. Jesus' total dependence on God was the glue that held together everything He said and did. Only doing what God told Him to do meant that whatever Jesus promised, God was bound to do.

If you're out on your own and make promises for God, then it's up to you to see them fulfilled. Whereas if God makes the promise through you, He will see it fulfilled. This is one of the reasons Jesus said to use His name in your requests to God. Jesus declared, "Ye have not chosen me, but I have chosen you, and ordained you, that ye should go and bring forth fruit, and *that* your fruit should remain: that whatsoever ye shall ask of the Father in my name, he may give it you" (John 15:16).

Key #2: Trustworthiness

You must be found trustworthy in the eyes of God to receive His promise of the blessing. Joseph was trustworthy with all that God had entrusted to him. Though his brothers hated him and sold him into slavery, Joseph still carried the favor of God's blessing on him. He wore it like the coat of many colors his father, Jacob, had given him (Gen. 37:3).

Because Joseph was trustworthy and carried the blessing of God with him, even as a slave he prospered. "And the LORD was with Joseph, and he was a prosperous man; and he was in the house of his master the Egyptian" (Gen. 39:2). Joseph was so prosperous that the master gave him charge of his entire estate.

When Joseph was in prison, he didn't trade the coat of God's blessing for that of a prisoner. Instead, in all that Joseph did, he prospered. So much so that even in the prison, Joseph became a trustee and overseer.

When Joseph was ushered into the presence of the king, the blessing of God went with him. He so blessed the king that soon Joseph was made second in command of all Egypt! Likewise, if you're not a slave to the devil, and you're wearing the garment of God's blessing, nothing can hold you down.

How did all this happen? Joseph was trustworthy to God and to the blessing of God upon him.

Key #3: Faithfulness

What does it mean to be faithful? Does it mean that you always...

- Show up to work on time and then work till the end of your shift?
- Give good measure, shaken down and pressed together in all that you do?
- Honor your husband or wife before others, even when they aren't around?

Being faithful means all of the above and more.

Abraham was a man of faith and is included among the great heroes of the faith recorded in Hebrews chapter 11. His faith not only drew him close to God, but enabled him to receive the blessing as recorded in Genesis 12:1-3.

Having faith is close akin to faithfulness – faith fullness. Being full of faith, then, is the engine that drives faithfulness. Therefore, when you are full of faith, you act upon that faith and bring the circumstances of your life in line with the faith of which you are full!

Too often, we look at our circumstances and wonder what we'll do. However, the faith-full declare what God will do about it according to the promises contained in His Word. Jesus said to speak to the mountain and it will be cast into the sea if you have faith (that is living) as a grain of muster seed (Matt. 17:20).

Being faithful to God's promises means you will direct your life according to them. You'll no longer be tossed about by the storms of life, because you'll be cruising on the luxury liner of God's blessing with the favor of God resting on you like Joseph's coat of many colors!

Believe To Receive

Jesus declared that mountains would be cast into the sea according to your faith. Well, it begins by believing God. Do you believe God will do what He says? If so, then do what God has established in His Word for you to do.

When Nehemiah returned to Jerusalem to rebuild the wall, he believed that God would fulfill the promises made through the prophets concerning Zion. Part of what was accomplished was the reinstitution of the feasts, offerings, and worship in the Temple that had been stopped because of the Jew's captivity. Because of Nehemiah's belief in God, he led the people into a covenant with God to rekindle their relationship with Him.

> And because of all this we make a sure *covenant*, and write *it*; and our princes, Levites, *and* priests, seal *unto it*…to bring the firstfruits of our ground, and the firstfruits of all fruit of all trees, year by year, unto the house of the LORD…
> (Neh. 9:38, 10:35)

Notice that one of the points of the covenant was about firstfruits and that from then on, they would be given year-by-year. This was done because the people believed God. They understood that holiness was just believing what God had said and patterning their lives after God's declaration.

Abraham believed God as well and it was counted to him as righteousness. We believe Jesus and have become the righteousness of God in Him (2 Cor. 5:21). Now, we step out like the Israelites of old to take God at His Word and receive according to His Word.

The Gift of Firstfruits

When you give firstfruits, you are giving of yourself even though your gift may be money. Abel gave of himself when he gave the firstlings of his flock. Cain gave of himself when he gave some of the fruit of the field. God gave an extension of Himself when He gave Jesus as firstfruits. Therefore, because your gift is an extension of you, it must be your best. Anything less and it will not be accepted.

God's blessing is the empowerment to have success in every area of your life. When you give your firstfruits and God accepts them, every area of your life is blessed. The Bible says that the blessing will rest on your house. "And the first of all the firstfruits of all *things*, and every oblation of all, of every *sort* of your oblations, shall be the priest's: ye shall also give unto the priest the first of your dough, that he may cause the blessing to rest in thine house" (Ezek 44:30)

Because the blessing is on your house, your entire household is blessed. Not only that, because it's blessed, it can't be cursed! You don't have to worry about the stuff of the world if your house is blessed. It can't touch your household. Sin has to go. Addiction has to go. Sickness has to go. All iniquity has to go. These can't remain in the holy presence of God in a blessed house.

Take hold of this truth. To obtain the blessing, you must position yourself to receive it. That's done through being obedient to God's Word, trusting God as your source and being trustworthy with what God's has given you, and being a faithful steward of all that God has placed in your care.

What are you going to do? Wait to see if someone you know gets blessed because of his or her obedience to firstfruits giving? Why don't you step out in obedient, trusting faith right now to take hold of your future and see your house blessed?

God's arms are outstretched – He's waiting for you.

CHAPTER 9

Blessed To Be A Blessing

—>•<—

Christ hath redeemed us from the curse of the law,
being made a curse for us: for it is written, Cursed is
every one that hangeth on a tree:
That the blessing of Abraham might come on the
Gentiles through Jesus Christ; that we might receive
the promise of the Spirit through faith.
(Gal. 3:13-14)

We learned in the last chapter that to receive God's promise
of blessing, one must live a life of obedience, trustworthiness and faithfulness. We also saw that the blessing promised was
the blessing of Abraham, or God's favor resting on one's life.

With God's favor resting on your life, you are blessed going in
and coming out (Deut. 28:6), and the blessings of God overtake
you. Your house is blessed and no curse can come upon you.

Furthermore, when the blessing of God is upon you, it is manifested in many ways: favor in your family, favor at work, favor in
the market, money, cars, houses, and more. However, the greatest
blessing of God's favor is your position to be used as His agent of
blessing in the world.

The Calling of Abraham

God searched far and wide in search of a man that He could trust. This man had to be a man of character and faithful with all that had been entrusted to him. Sadly, throughout the generations on earth, all were idol worshipers and none worshiped God.

However, there was a man in Ur of the Chaldees who, though an idol worshiper, was faithful to the revelation given him. Therefore, God tapped him on the shoulder and said, "Get thee out of thy country, and from thy kindred, and from thy father's house, unto a land that I will shew thee" (Gen. 12:1). When this man heard the voice of the true God, he left his idols behind and embarked on a journey of faith that completely changed his life and spawned nations.

This man's name was Abram, which God later changed to Abraham, the father of multitudes. There are several men in the Scriptures who are types of Jesus, but Abraham is the only man who is a type of God the Father. Abraham so loved God as to give up his only son, Isaac.

Living in faithful obedience to God brought Abraham into a level of communion with the Father unsurpassed by most men or women. "Abraham believed God, and it was imputed unto him for righteousness: and he was called the Friend of God" (James 2:23).

The Lord directed this man of faith and obedience to leave his land and countrymen and go to a place that God would show him. In faith, Abraham obeyed God. Out of that obedience, God declared:

> And I will make of thee a great nation, and I will bless thee, and make thy name great; and thou shalt be a blessing:

And I will bless them that bless thee, and curse him
that curseth thee: and in thee shall all families of the
earth be blessed.
(Gen. 12:2-3)

The Blessing of Abraham

When God's blessing was bestowed upon Abraham, great
power and authority came to him. According to the Scripture, God
promised to make of Abraham a great nation and that his name
would be great. God also declared that He would bless whomever
blessed Abraham and would curse whomever cursed Abraham.

God in essence told Abraham that he was God's agent on the
earth. This stewardship parallels the declaration God made in
Genesis 1:26 giving man dominion over the earth to subdue it. God
granted to Abraham the right to exercise His authority on the earth
and be the vessel of blessing to mankind.

The promise of blessing given to Abraham still had to be lived
out day-by-day. Some of the promise was realized right away, but
much of it stretched far beyond Abraham's lifetime.

Seven Points of God's Blessing

God's promised blessing was outlined in seven points that
touched every aspect of Abraham's life. Each of these points could
be a chapter in another book, but we'll just look briefly at each one
now. God declared:

1. I will make of thee a great nation.

2. I will bless thee.
3. I will…make thy name great.
4. Thou shalt be a blessing.
5. I will bless them that bless thee.
6. I will curse them that curse thee.
7. In thee shall all the families of the earth be blessed.

These points make up the blessing of Abraham and are promised to us as well (compare Deut. 28:1-14). Firstfruits giving brings us into alignment with God according to our faith to unlock these seven points of blessing.

Kingdom Living Means Kingdom Blessing

Remember, the blessing isn't cars, boats, houses, or money. Those things can at best only be a sign of the blessing. The blessing of God transcends the abundance of things and it rests on you to launch you into another realm of God's Kingdom.

Jesus said to seek first the Kingdom of God and His righteousness and everything else would be added to you (Matt. 6:33). Seeking God's Kingdom before all else means you have died to your wants and are seeking only what God wants. This attitude of living opens the windows of Heaven to bless everyone around you. This is what it means to have the blessing rest in your house (Eze. 44:38).

God created everyone, not just someone. Knowing this also means knowing that God desires all of His creation to be blessed – He wants none left out. When a person takes hold of this knowledge and understands that God's blessing goes beyond being saved, they begin to see what God can and will do. As the church takes hold of it, entire communities are changed by the presence of God manifested in the lives of people committed to Him.

Do you want to see your family changed? Live a Kingdom life. Do you want to see your workplace changed? Live a Kingdom life. Do you want to see your community changed? You guessed it. Live a Kingdom life!

Living a Kingdom life means giving freely of what God has given you. You are blessed to be a blessing. God entrusted you with His riches because He knows you'll not hoard it for yourself. Instead, you'll see a need that God sees and when He instructs, fill it. Kingdom living means being able to…

- sow generously into worthwhile Kingdom causes to see the Gospel of Jesus Christ spread around the world
- give away a car to someone who needs it as God directs.
- bless someone with a house because you know God said do it.
- be the largest giver in your church.

These are only a few examples of Kingdom giving based on Kingdom living. Many more can be brought before you, but you can see that Kingdom living is not about stuff – it's about ministering to others and using all the resources that God has promised to do it.

The Blessing of Faith

Abraham was blessed with faith as well. As he saw God move, his faith was strengthened and he moved all the more in step with God's plan. Likewise, as you see God move, you'll be excited to move out in God's plan. Firstfruits giving is part of that plan.

As you give your firstfruits, you prophetically declare God's plan and purpose over your substance. This prophetic declaration puts in motion a series of events in the heavenlies that change the value of what you've given. Remember, the firstfruits is the best of whatever you're giving.

Therefore, if you give the first $50 of a $200 per month raise, you are prophetically declaring God's purpose and plan over that raise. Remember, Nehemiah declared that firstfruits were to be given year-by-year, so for the remainder of the year, that raise is filled with God's potential and purpose.

As you give, God moves in and strengthens your faith. He knows, like you do, that faith is an action word. James wrote that faith without works is dead (James 2:26). When faith is exercised in God's direction, the purpose of God flows out to meet that faith and builds it up in strength. The more you exercise your faith, the stronger it grows, becoming more like the faith of God. The question then becomes, "How much should I give?" instead of, "How much should I keep?"

Declaring Your Firstfruits

You decide what your firstfruit offering will be. God has given some guidelines in Scripture, but the final decision is left up to you.

There is a story in Scripture about a king who wanted to defeat an army that was attacking the nation. The king went before the prophet of the Lord to inquire about the situation and received this word:

> And Elisha said unto him, Take bow and arrows.
> And he took unto him bow and arrows.
> And he said to the king of Israel, Put thine hand

upon the bow. And he put his hand *upon it*: and Elisha put his hands upon the king's hands.

And he said, Open the window eastward. And he opened *it*. Then Elisha said, Shoot. And he shot. And he said, The arrow of the LORD'S deliverance, and the arrow of deliverance from Syria: for thou shalt smite the Syrians in Aphek, till thou have consumed *them*.

And he said, Take the arrows. And he took *them*. And he said unto the king of Israel, Smite upon the ground. And he smote thrice, and stayed.

And the man of God was wroth with him, and said, Thou shouldest have smitten five or six times; then hadst thou smitten Syria till thou hadst consumed *it*: whereas now thou shalt smite Syria *but* thrice.

(2 Kings 13:15-19)

Notice that the king was assured victory in only three battles in accordance with his obedience to the Word of the Lord. Elisha declared that if he had struck the ground five or six times, Syria would have been completely defeated.

Giving firstfruits is like this story of the king. Remember, giving firstfruits is a prophetic declaration unto the Lord about what He is going to do, not an offering giving thanks for what God has already done.

What are you going to declare as your firstfruits? The declaration you make determines your stance of faith. Will you, like Abraham, stake it all on the Word of God, or will you, like the king of Israel, only strike the ground three times and think it's enough?

Give Your Best As Firstfruits

Throughout this teaching, we've emphasized the importance of the firstfruits being your best. Paul declared, "For if the firstfruit *be* holy, the lump *is* also *holy*: and if the root *be* holy, so *are* the branches" (Rom. 11:16). Therefore, if your firstfruits are unholy, then the lump will be unholy. As is the root, so goes the branch.

As you give your best, God will do likewise. Scripture teaches us to treat our neighbors like we want them to treat us (Lev. 19:18; Matt. 7:12; 22:39). This principle also applies in our relationship with God. Yes. God is loving and benevolent, but if you choose to give Him your worst instead of your best, you stand in danger of judgment (Matt. 25:14-30). Furthermore, how can you expect to receive God's best when you give your worst?

God's desire is to bless and not curse, to bring life and not death. He is your loving Father, and He's waiting for you to speak to your future and declare His promises over your seed and your seed's seed. Your prophetic declaration made through firstfruits giving brings honor to both you and God as you step out in faith to believe Him and take Him at His Word.

Firstfruits Sown – Holy Increase Reaped – Blessing Others

Look unto God now and begin to declare your firstfruits. Give them to the priest so he can wave them before the Lord as a holy offering, sanctified unto God. Sow generously so you can reap generously and begin to live large in the Lord. Don't look at the past, look to the future and seek what God will do in and through you.

I assure you, by the promises of God spoken in the Bible that every Word will come to pass. Including those promises that relate to you about being a blessing to others around you. The blessing will rest on your house. God's favor will be in, around and through you, affecting all that you do.

However, it's up to you to believe God. Abraham did and look at what God did through him. Imagine what God can do in and through you, as you are obedient and faithful to Him. Listen to the Lord as He challenges you to step out in faith:

> ...prove me now herewith, saith the LORD of hosts, if I will not open you the windows of heaven, and pour you out a blessing, that *there shall* not *be room* enough *to receive it.*
>
> And I will rebuke the devourer for your sakes, and he shall not destroy the fruits of your ground; neither shall your vine cast her fruit before the time in the field, saith the LORD of hosts (Mal 3:10-11). Just like you ought to prove God in tithes and offering, chose this day to prove Him in firstfruits giving.

Epilogue

The purpose of this book is to help Believers understand that God's desire is to see them walk in His blessing. I've tried to explain in twenty thousand words what I taught over nine weeks in much greater detail using more than fifty thousand words.

To complete this teaching, let's briefly review the major points covered by each chapter.

Point #1: The Truth About Firstfruits

Firstfruits giving is an expression of dependence on God unlike any other offering. Giving firstfruits makes a declaration that more is on the way. Too often, we give out of obligation instead of anticipation. Firstfruits giving shatters that mindset and focuses our attention on God and God's promises.

Giving firstfruits honors God by declaring that he is in charge of your future. Think of it like this: When you buy something on credit, you are gambling that you'll have the money in the future to pay for what you've charged. Giving a firstfruits offering recognizes that God has set a harvest in your life that He is overseeing. It's the opposite of buying on credit and hoping something will be there to pay the bill. Firstfruits giving establishes the future in prosperity whereas credit robs you of your future increase.

The Bible declares that we must seek God and His Kingdom in all that we do (Matt. 6:33). As we do so, the promise is that everything will be added to us that we need. Jesus made it very clear in the Sermon on the Mount (Matt. 5-7) that we must not worry about tomorrow. Too much debt causes us to worry about where the money will come from to fulfill our obligations. Jesus further said that we couldn't serve both God and mammon (Matt. 6:24). Therefore, our responsibility is to God first. As we seek Him and His righteousness our needs are met and mammon (debt) is brought under control.

Point #2: A Higher Level of Giving

Giving your firstfruits opens windows of heaven that may have remained shut even though you were faithful in the tithe. It's a different, higher level of giving than even the tithe. Firstfruit giving means that instead of looking at the harvest after it's been gathered in, you look at the harvest before it's even come in – and then give on it!

Giving firstfruits leads you into prophetic giving based on what you see God doing, not what you want Him to do. When you begin to give prophetically, you open yourself to realms of God's glory that embolden you even more. You begin to see that no matter how much you give in obedience to God, you can never out-give Him.

You also begin to see what you've sown bear fruit. Too often, Believers give so they can see a building built. Prophetic giving opens the realm of seeing cities and nations changed for God. God is glorified as He magnifies your firstfruits to bring about His purpose on earth.

Higher levels of giving lead to higher levels of living. Begin in submission with the tithe, and God will move you toward giving offerings. Stay in submission with tithes and offerings, and God will move you toward giving of the firstfruits. When that happens, look out! God is positioning you to receive more than you could imagine. The apostle Paul declared that if you can think about it, it's not God's best: "Now unto him that is able to do exceeding abundantly above all that we ask or think…" (Eph. 3:20).

Point #3: Faith Overcomes Fear

Trust leads to love, which then leads to faith. Faith, then, overcomes fear. This is true because love is such an integral part of faith. The Bible declares that, "perfect love casteth out all fear." Perfect love and faith cannot be separated – they are integral to each other. When love is present and faith is exercised, things happen.

We've seen that firstfruit giving is different than tithing and other offerings. Tithing and other offerings honor what God has already done, whereas firstfruits honor what God is going to do! Remember, giving firstfruits is prophetically declaring the remainder of the harvest. Prophetic giving is the highest level of giving possible. When you give your firstfruits offering, you make a prophetic declaration that the balance is holy!

This declaration is given out of trust, love and reverence to God. Your faith in God enables you to give firstfruits. If you have faith in your boss and trust in the world, and decide to give the first part of your raise to a lottery, you are gambling on what the world can give. However, giving firstfruits out of faith to God and love for Him is a declaration that your future is secure in Him!

Point #4: God's Firstfruit Offering

God offered His Son, Jesus, as His firstfruits offering thus making available some exciting promises. Paul wrote in Romans 11:16, "For if the firstfruit *be* holy, the lump *is* also *holy*: and if the root *be* holy, so *are* the branches." We know that because Jesus is the Son of God that, as firstfruits, He is holy. Therefore, as we are found in Him through our confession of faith, we, the lump, are declared holy as well!

God's declaration of our holiness comes not from what we've done or how good we are, but through the finished work of Jesus on the cross at Calvary. Paul wrote: "Therefore if any man *be* in Christ, *he is* a new creature: old things are passed away; behold, all things are become new" (2 Cor. 5:17). Our status as a new creature is secured through Jesus and His standing as the firstfruits of God. This truth of redemption places us back into the Paradise of God, thus making our election sure.

Point #5: The Firstfruits of Self

God desires the best from you. He gave you His best; now give Him your best. Offer yourself to Him as a clean, holy, firstfruit offering.

When Jesus was crucified, a Roman soldier was attending at the foot of the cross, waiting for Jesus to die. When Jesus cried out and gave up His Spirit, the soldier declared, "Certainly this was a righteous man" (Luke 23:47).

What would someone who didn't know you say in a similar circumstance? Would they be able to tell that your life was different because of what the Lord Jesus had done in and through you?

We live in a convenience society: Fast food, express lanes, drive-through banking and church on TV. However, living the Christian life is not convenient. In fact, it's often down right inconvenient. The demand of righteousness means we live to a higher standard and march to a different drummer. Our call is heavenward, not earthbound.

Point #6: The Power in Your Hands

Seed in a barn does the farmer no good. It must be released into the earth. The great thing about first fruit giving is that this awesome power is in your hands. It is not left up to someone else to determine your ability to lay claim to this blessing from God. As you prepare to sow firstfruits offerings, make ready your heart. The Bible declares that, "The heart *is* deceitful above all *things*, and desperately wicked" (Jer. 17:9). Therefore, examine your heart and get it right with God.

Sowing for the blessing requires a pure heart. Cain's heart was darkened toward God and his offering was rejected. Likewise, Ananias and Sapphira came before the Lord with deceitful hearts and were stricken dead. Purify your heart and come openly before the Lord. The promise given to Cain is just as valid today as it was thousands of years ago: "If thou doest well, shalt thou not be accepted?" (Gen. 4:7).

You may not have billions of dollars to give as a firstfruits offering, but you have something. You decide in your heart what to give – there is no prescribed amount. Paul declared, "Every man according as he purposeth in his heart, *so let him give*; not grudgingly, or of necessity: for God loveth a cheerful giver" (2 Cor. 9:7). See the importance of the heart? You give according to what you purpose in it.

Point #7: Breakthrough Power

God wants you to take the responsibility for commanding your breakthrough. You command breakthrough by speaking God's

Word. You can't just have it in your heart you've got to speak it as well. This is of primary importance, especially in firstfruits giving. The Bible says that you must make a statement as you sow your firstfruits. This statement is your prophetic utterance of what God will do in and through you.

When you give and declare your firstfruits it honors God. You are conveying to God that you know that it was He who brought you out of the kingdom of darkness into the kingdom of his dear Son. God has lead you from the land of not enough (Egypt), through the land of just enough (the wilderness), to the land of more than enough (the promised land). Therefore, you give unto God the firstfruit so that the blessing will come to your house."

By declaring before God, you set in motion the laws of blessing and prosperity. You become like the ambassador who is perfectly representing the king. You begin to walk in favor before God and man like you've never walked before. You begin commanding your own breakthrough!

Point #8: Receive Your Promise

When you give firstfruits, you are giving of yourself even though your gift may be money. Abel gave of himself when he gave the firstlings of his flock. Cain gave of himself when he gave some of the fruit of the field. God gave an extension of Himself when He gave Jesus as firstfruits. Therefore, because your gift is an extension of you, it must be your best. Anything less and it will not be accepted.

God's blessing is the empowerment to have success in every area of your life. When you give your firstfruits and God accepts them, every area of your life is blessed. The Bible says that the blessing will rest on your house. "And the first of all the firstfruits of all *things*, and every oblation of all, of every *sort* of your oblations, shall be the priest's: ye shall also give unto the priest the first of your dough, that he may cause the blessing to rest in thine house" (Ezek 44:30)

Because the blessing is on your house, your entire household is blessed. Not only that, because it's blessed, it can't be cursed! You don't have to worry about the stuff of the world if your house is blessed. It can't touch your household. Sin has to go. Addiction has to go. Sickness has to go. All iniquity has to go. These can't remain in the holy presence of God in a blessed house.

Take hold of this truth. To obtain the blessing, you must position yourself to receive it. That's done through being obedient to God's Word, trusting God as your source and being trustworthy with what God's has given you, and being a faithful steward of all that God has placed in your care.

Point #9: Blessed To Be A Blessing

Jesus said to seek first the Kingdom of God and His righteousness and everything else would be added to you (Matt. 6:33). Seeking God's Kingdom before all else means you have died to your wants and are seeking only what God wants. This attitude of living opens the windows of Heaven to bless everyone around you. This is what it means to have the blessing rest in your house (Eze. 44:38).

God created everyone, not just someone. Knowing this also means knowing that God desires all of His creation to be blessed – He wants none left out. When a person takes hold of this knowledge and understands that God's blessing goes beyond being saved, they begin to see what God can and will do. As the church takes hold of it, entire communities are changed by the presence of God manifested in the lives of people committed to Him.

Do you want to see your family changed? Live a Kingdom life. Do you want to see your workplace changed? Live a Kingdom life. Do you want to see your community changed? You guessed it. Live a Kingdom life!

Living a Kingdom life means giving freely of what God has given you. You are blessed to be a blessing. God entrusted you with His riches because He knows you'll not hoard it for yourself. Instead, you'll see a need or a desire the way God sees it and when He instructs you will fill it.

The decision is yours to make. Take hold of this teaching and believe God to fulfill His Word. I promise you that if you do, your life will be forever changed.

Printed in the United States
75513LV00002B/82-279